Cover design and layout by: Richard Joosten Design, Toronto   www.joostendesign.com

Canadian Cataloguing In Publication Data
Fisher, Douglas P.
Canadian Restaurant Accounting
ISBN 978-0-9811878-1-5

1.   Restaurant and foodservice accounting
2.   Bookkeeping
3.   Internal controls
4.   Restaurant valuations

Published and distributed by Canadian Restaurant and Foodservices Association
316 Bloor Street West
Toronto, Ontario, Canada M5S 1W5
1-800-387-5649
info@crfa.ca
www.crfa.ca

Douglas P. Fisher can be reached at 416-489-6996 or email at doug@fhgi.com or through the FHG International Inc. web site at www.fhgi.com

Printed and bound in Canada

Accounting
Standards Board

AcSB

CNC

Conseil des normes
comptables

FOREWORD

July 2009

Generally accepted accounting principles in Canada are formulated by
the Accounting Standards Board. In developing principles, the Board
recognizes that no rule of general application can be phrased to suit all
circumstances and that professional judgment must be exercised
in determining what constitutes fair presentation or good practice in
particular circumstances.

The Canadian Restaurant and Foodservices Association (CRFA) has
published Canadian Restaurant Accounting to provide practical guidance
for applying accounting principles to Canadian restaurants and food
service enterprises. Guidance is provided on a wide range of accounting
topics that are of particular interest to the industry.

The initiative of CRFA in publishing this guidance is welcomed as a
useful contribution to enhancing the quality of financial reporting in
Canada.

Peter Martin

Peter Martin, CA
Director,
Accounting Standards

Table of contents

Table of exhibits

Acknowledgements

We appreciate the opportunity of preparing *Canadian Restaurant Accounting* for publication by the Canadian Restaurant and Foodservices Association (CRFA). First published under the name *Canadian Restaurant Accounting & Internal Controls*, in 1993, these standards have been widely adopted by the industry as "THE" book on Canadian restaurant accounting standards. The book reflects our knowledge and experience, and outlines our ideas on the financial accounts and internal control systems that should be maintained in the restaurant and foodservice industry.

Several people were involved in helping me draft the original copy in the early 1990s, including Manlio Marescotti, Carla Daum, Phil Forester, and the late Debbie Baker.

This updated version brings forth all the significant changes to generally accepted accounting principles (GAAP) as they affect the industry, and includes updated and more comprehensive internal controls. We have also added a short chapter on restaurant valuations that can be used as a guideline in establishing a restaurant's fair market value for financing, selling or purchasing.

We have worked hard to ensure that all the information provided is of the highest standard. Marvin B. Martenfeld, FCA, Partner and Yogesh Jani, Senior Manager of Collins Barrow, reviewed the book from an accounting point of view to ensure its conformity to GAAP, its relevance, and ease of use.

I would also like to thank Jill Holroyd, Sandra de Crescenzo and Griff Tripp for their invaluable assistance in the production of this book.

Yours very truly,
FHG INTERNATIONAL INC.
Foodservice & Franchise Consultants

Per: Douglas P. Fisher, BAS, MSc, CFE, FCSI
        Fellow Certified Management Consultant
        Fellow Hostelry Institute
        President

Introduction

There has long been a need for developing an accounting format and approach that both address the specific needs of Canadian restaurants and conform with generally accepted accounting principles (GAAP), developed by the Accounting Standards Board. These standards are intended to simplify the bookkeeping and preparation of financial statements for restaurants. The statements are designed to provide management with pertinent financial information, allow for easy analysis of financial performance and for comparison of data and ratios within the industry. The CRFA has been using these standards since 1993 as a basis for monitoring the industry and reporting industry financial statistics.

The internal control systems described in this book are adaptable throughout the foodservice industry and can be used by all restaurants irrespective of theme, type of service and size. Restaurateurs must implement control systems in today's tough economic environment, in order to ensure their restaurant's profitability, and ultimately, survival. The internal controls contained in this book are easy to implement and monitor, and address the food, beverage and labour areas. These areas typically represent the largest expenses for restaurants and are subject to significant fluctuations if not rigidly controlled.

Canadian Restaurant Accounting addresses the needs of independent, chain and franchise operators, and provides direction for the preparation and interpretation of financial statements. This book will also be beneficial to other foodservice operators including caterers, contract food suppliers and institutional foodservice operators. While some of the financial statements may have to be modified to meet the specific needs of these operators, the book provides a framework for comprehensive financial reporting and internal control systems. *Canadian Restaurant Accounting* should be used in conjunction with a basic accounting textbook that discusses all the bookkeeping details required to keep financial records.

The book does not deal with consolidated financial statements and, therefore, is not a strong reference source to operators who require consolidated financial statements. However, this book will provide these operators with a basic reporting format to use and follow which will allow them to compare operating units within any one, or a multitude of, restaurant operations.

Canadian Restaurant Accounting is divided into four chapters for easy reference.

Chapter One discusses four major financial statements:

- ➤ *Income statement*, which reports revenues and expenses for a reporting period.

- ➤ *Balance sheet*, which details the restaurant's assets and liabilities at a specific point in time.

➤ *Statement of retained earnings*, which details the increases and decreases in retained earnings during the reporting period.

➤ *Statement of cash flow*, which reflects the cash generated and cash spent by the restaurant and how it financed its operations in a reporting period.

This chapter also discusses related aspects of financial statements, including:

➤ *Notes to the financial statements;*

➤ *Financial projections*; and,

➤ *Operating ratios.*

Chapter Two details a process for tracking the restaurant's revenues (sales) and expenses (costs) for a reporting period. The chapter describes how to set up the books of account, which include the supporting journals and ledgers needed to prepare financial statements. While it may not be practical, or necessary, for management to prepare financial statements, it is important that they understand the process. Management should know how the financial information is tabulated and be able to understand the statements in order to better control the restaurant's day-to-day operation. While most, if not all, bookkeeping is completed electronically, it is important for the restaurant operator to understand the methodology that has been used to monitor their income and expenses, enabling them to get to the financial root of any problem that may occur.

Chapter Three details a series of internal controls designed specifically for restaurants. A section is dedicated to each of the prime cost areas of food, beverage and labour. In addition, there is a section on cash controls. Each section has a series of detailed control methodologies, which can be easily implemented and used in all foodservice operations.

Chapter Four provides a basic approach to restaurant valuations. Over the years we have found that many operators are unsure as to the worth of their restaurant business in the open market. We have decided to add a process by which a restaurant operator can value their business. Operators, banks, or valuators can effectively find a realistic value for a restaurant using this valuation approach. The concepts outlined in this chapter will be to value an independent restaurant operation. The approach outlined cannot be effectively used to value consolidated businesses nor major corporate entities. Valuations of consolidated restaurant companies and public companies are best conducted by professionals as the methodologies become significantly more complex than those outlined herein.

The Appendix lists a chart of accounts, which can be adapted by any restaurant to record and track revenue and expense data.

The financial statements shown in this book are for illustrative purposes only. Operating ratios are typical of those found in the industry but should not be used as the basis for assessing a restaurant's financial performance.

Chapter One

Financial Statement Reporting

This chapter will provide restaurant management with an understanding of the importance of financial statements, and how the information contained in the statements can be used to improve the restaurant's profitability.

The chapter provides a format for preparing financial statements that highlights important operating ratios and allows for comparison within the industry. Each financial statement is discussed in detail, beginning with the purpose of the statement, followed by a comprehensive description of each line item. An example of each financial statement is provided for illustrative purposes.

Exhibit 1 details the accounting process for a restaurant in a flowchart format. The flowchart shows how the daily transactions are tracked and recorded in the books of account and ultimately reported in the financial statements. The books of account record business transactions as they occur and group the transactions according to the chart of accounts (detailed in Appendix). Chapter Two outlines the basic books of account system that was developed for the restaurant industry, and which is easy to set up and maintain.

The following types of financial statements are generally prepared for a restaurant:

- ➤ Income statement;
- ➤ Balance sheet;
- ➤ Statement of retained earnings; and,
- ➤ Statement of cash flow.

Exhibit 1
Accounting Flow Chart

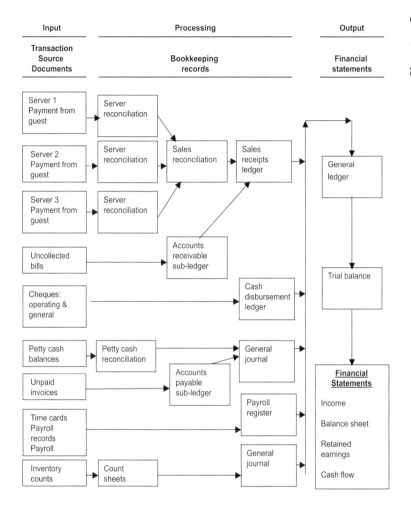

Input	Processing	Output
Transaction Source Documents	Bookkeeping records	Financial statements

Financial statements to be provided to parties external to the business should be prepared according to Canadian generally accepted accounting principles (GAAP). It is the purpose of *Canadian Restaurant Accounting* to provide detailed explanation, specific to the restaurant and foodservice industry, on how to prepare financial statements, within the framework of Canadian GAAP.

The main source of GAAP in Canada is the *Canadian Institute of Chartered Accountants Handbook*. The *CICA Handbook* contains many specific recommendations on financial reporting. GAAP continually changes and this guide is only current to the date it was published. Readers will need to refer to the current version of the *CICA Handbook* to ensure full compliance with GAAP as of a date subsequent to publication. As a general requirement, the financial statements, including notes, should contain "any information required for fair presentation of financial position, results of operations or cash flows."

Users of financial statements

Financial statements are prepared to meet the information needs of several different types of users. Who these users are and what they expect to learn from a set of financial statements is summarized below.

Management

Financial statements provide information on the restaurant's performance and financial situation that management can use to make more sound business decisions. The statements are an important tool in controlling the restaurant's operations in order to track sales, monitor costs and maximize profitability. Additionally, financial statements can be used to compare results between reporting periods. A reporting period is defined as the time period covered by the financial statements and can be, for example, for a period of four weeks, month, quarter, or year(s). Ratio analysis, discussed later in this chapter, can help management identify problem areas within the restaurant.

Financial statements are essential to management in budgeting and planning for the future. Projected statements (budgets) can be compared to actual results and provide a basis for evaluating the restaurant's financial performance. Budgeting is an important management tool and is discussed in greater detail later in this chapter.

The **income statement** allows management to assess the restaurant's operating performance by detailing the revenues and expenses for a reporting period.

The **balance sheet** provides an overview of the restaurant's financial situation by summarizing all of the restaurant's assets, liabilities and shareholders' equity at a point in time.

The **statement of cash flow** tracks how much cash was received, where it came from, and what the cash was spent on. The statement will assist its readers to evaluate the restaurant's liquidity and solvency.

Investors and/or shareholders

Investors and/or shareholders have a financial stake in the business. Accordingly, they should have access to financial statements in order to assess how the restaurant is performing, and determine their return on investment (ROI).

Creditors and bankers

Creditors and bankers will often require financial statements in conjunction with the initial credit or loan granting process and possibly on a regular basis thereafter. Financiers and bankers will want to monitor the security of their loan, and the restaurant's ability to generate sufficient cash flow to meet its financial obligations.

Government/Canada Revenue Agency (CRA)

There are many government regulations that require a restaurant to prepare adequate books of account and financial statements. Best practice for filing a restaurant's annual income tax return is to provide financial statements prepared following Canadian generally accepted accounting principles (GAAP).

Financial records are also used to support remittances for payroll deductions, provincial sales taxes (PST), goods and services tax (GST), and harmonized sales tax (HST).

Frequency for preparing financial statements

Restaurants should prepare financial statements on a periodic basis throughout the year. In order to closely monitor operating performance, the income statement should be prepared either every month or four-week period. The advantage of using a four-week period (as opposed to month) is that it provides management with 13 equal periods throughout the year and, thus, comparable data for analyzing results and identifying trends between reporting periods. The advantage of preparing monthly statements is that it is easier to account for various monthly expenses (e.g. rent, loan payments, phone). These expenses would otherwise have to be allocated to two different periods (for example, 28/31 of the month's expense to the current four-week period and 3/31 of the expense to the next period).

It is beneficial to management if the balance sheet, statement of retained earnings and a statement of cash flow can also be prepared, if not at the end of each month or four-week period, then at least quarterly. The benefits of preparing these statements are that they will provide management with the ability to evaluate the restaurant's overall financial situation. This evaluation will allow management to identify, and react to, problems with regards to the restaurant's liquidity and solvency. Periodic statements will also facilitate the preparation of year-end statements.

It is important that management develops a reporting schedule, which details when financial statements should be produced (e.g. every four weeks, quarterly). Efforts should be made to ensure that financial statements are produced as close to the end of the reporting period as possible (within four to five days). Having this timely information will allow management to identify problem areas and immediately take the appropriate action(s).

Basic accounting concepts

When preparing financial statements for restaurants, certain basic accounting concepts must be followed. A brief discussion of these concepts follows.

Accrual accounting

The accounting model for a restaurant is based on accounting for all transactions as they are incurred. A transaction is the exchange of a good or service for a specified amount of consideration, normally money. Therefore, a period's income statement should account for all expenses and revenues incurred in the period irrespective of whether cash has been received and/or paid. This results in a proper matching of revenues and expenses to properly monitor performance.

Examples of common transactions in the restaurant business include:

- ➤ customer purchase of food or beverage;
- ➤ costs of food or beverage served;
- ➤ employee wages; and,
- ➤ rent.

Revenue recognition

The accounting model has some specific rules about when revenue is considered earned (recognized) and, therefore, can be reported in the restaurant's financial statements.

Determining when revenue has been earned is normally a straightforward matter. When a meal has been served to a customer and the customer pays the bill, revenue has been earned. This is the case even if the customer pays on some sort of a credit basis, usually a credit card. The process of converting the customer's credit into cash is an issue of accounts receivable collection.

Matching concept

The matching concept is a cause-and-effect relationship where all expenses related to the production and sale of a good or service (a meal) are matched to its sale.

The income statement reports income and expenses on an accrual basis. Thus, sales are included as earned, even though the cash may not yet have been collected, and expenses are included as incurred, even though they have not yet been paid. Accordingly, in restaurants, all expenses associated with preparing and serving a meal are included in the same financial reporting period as when the revenue (sale) is reported.

In order to achieve a proper matching of revenues and expenses it is often necessary to make adjustments to the financial records, prior to preparing the financial statements. For example, the insurance expense for the reporting period is based on the number of months in the period as opposed to the amount paid out during the period. Therefore, if the reporting period is nine months long, three-quarters of the annual insurance premium (nine of 12 months) must be charged to that reporting period.

Double-entry accounting

Transactions are recorded in the books of account through the use of double-entry accounting. Under double-entry accounting the restaurant's balance sheet must balance so that assets equal the sum of liabilities and shareholders' equity.

Each transaction that the restaurant enters into will have two sides (a debit and a credit) and will affect at least two different accounts. For example, the payment of wages to an employee is a single transaction. However, that single transaction requires that an entry be made in two accounts:

> ➤ 'cash' is credited (reduced by the amount of the wages).

> ➤ 'salaries, wages and benefits' is debited (increased by the amount of the wages).

The double-entry accounting system is a self-checking system. If it has not been properly adhered to, then the balance sheet will not balance.

Business entity concept

For accounting purposes a restaurant is considered a distinct business entity from its owners or shareholders. This is whether the restaurant is a sole proprietorship, a partnership or an incorporated entity. Thus, the assets and liabilities of the restaurant are accounted for separately from those of its owners or shareholders.

Comparative analysis

In order to comply with GAAP, financial statements must present comparative figures for the previous period. For example, a restaurant's financial statements for the second year of operation (20x2) would present for each line item the applicable figure for 20x2 and 20x1 (e.g. sales-food in 20x2 and 20x1). This concept is illustrated in Exhibits 2, 3, 4, and 5.

Management responsibility

Management is responsible for the contents of the financial statements and their accuracy. Factually incorrect financial statements (e.g. where revenue is understated or expenses are overstated) are the sole responsibility of the restaurant's officers and directors.

Income Statement

The purpose of the income statement, illustrated in Exhibit 2, is to report on the income generated (revenues less expenses) from business transactions which occurred in the reporting period. A reporting period is the time period covered by the financial statements. The income statement heading indicates length and the last day of the period, and the revenues and expenses reported in the statement are for all transactions incurred up to the end of business on that date. The income statement allows management to assess the financial performance of the restaurant and to analyze the revenues and expenses (either as a dollar figure or as a percentage of sales) for the period.

Throughout the year, income statements should be prepared every four weeks, or month. At the end of the fiscal year an income statement is prepared for the entire year and is, in essence, a summary of all the four-week, or monthly, income statements.

The revenue and expense information used to prepare the income statement comes from the books of account, which are discussed in Chapter Two.

The most common way of analyzing revenues and expenses is to examine the item as a percentage of gross sales. All items are taken as a percentage of gross sales except for:

- ➤ food cost percent (calculated as a percentage of food sales);

- ➤ beverage cost percent (calculated as a percentage of beverage sales); and,

- ➤ sundry costs percent (calculated as a percentage of sundry sales).

Using the percentage figures as the basis for an analysis allows for easy and meaningful comparison between reporting periods and industry averages. The percentage figures should be shown on the income statement to the right of the line item's dollar value.

Exhibit 2

Income Statement

SAMPLE RESTAURANT
Income Statement
For the year ended December 31, 20x2

SALES	20x2		20x1	
Food	$1,240,482	77.0%	$1,197,428	78.0%
Beverage	304,482	18.9%	301,873	19.7%
Sundry	66,052	4.1%	35,000	2.3%
TOTAL SALES	1,611,016	100.0%	1,534,301	100.0%
COST OF SALES				
Food	421,764	34.0%	408,551	34.1%
Beverage	109,005	35.8%	108,943	36.1%
Sundry	29,856	45.2%	15,500	44.3%
TOTAL COST OF SALES	560,625	34.8%	532,994	34.7%
GROSS MARGIN	1,050,391	65.2%	1,001,307	65.3%
EXPENSES				
Salaries, Wages				
& Benefits	512,303	31.8%	479,520	31.3%
Occupancy	134,871	8.4%	128,449	8.4%
Operating	83,945	5.2%	76,971	5.0%
General & Administrative	49,941	3.1%	48,735	3.2%
Marketing	45,108	2.8%	39,840	2.6%
Entertainment	14,499	0.9%	15,340	1.0%
Royalty Fees	0	0.0%	0	0.0%
TOTAL EXPENSES	840,667	52.2%	788,855	51.4%
OPERATING INCOME	209,724	13.0%	212,452	13.8%
INTEREST (Note 3)	10,550	0.7%	11,700	0.8%
DEPRECIATION	81,551	5.1%	98,428	6.4%
INCOME BEFORE TAX	117,623	7.3%	102,324	6.7%
INCOME TAX	29,406	1.8%	25,581	1.7%
NET INCOME	$88,217	5.5%	$76,743	5.0%

(see accompanying notes to financial statements)

When analyzing expenses, management should differentiate between variable and fixed costs. Variable costs vary with the volume of business and can be controlled to a greater extent than fixed costs. Cost of food sales, for instance, is a variable cost that varies directly with food sales. When analyzing variable costs, management should examine the operating ratio (expense / total sales = percent), as opposed to the dollar value.

Fixed costs remain the same regardless of the volume of business. For example, interest on a bank loan has to be paid, regardless of the level of sales. Fixed costs are of less day-to-day concern to management as they cannot be directly controlled in the short-term.

Format of the income statement

The income statement illustrated previously is in a basic format that can be used by most restaurants. Depending on the type of operation, and the level of information required by the users, it might be necessary to make some minor modifications to this format. In cases where more detailed information is required it is preferable to include this additional information in supporting schedules. Management should carefully assess the need for this additional information as the schedules are time consuming to complete and may be too detailed to easily analyze.

The income statement is broken into the following categories:

- ➤ 'Sales' are reported at the top of the statement and are broken down by major sources of revenue (food, beverage and sundry).

- ➤ The 'cost of sales' is reported underneath and is broken down in similar categories to 'sales'.

- ➤ The 'gross margin' equals the net amount of 'sales' less the 'cost of sales'.

- ➤ The expenses associated with running the restaurant are itemized below the 'gross margin' by major category type under the heading 'expenses'. The 'gross margin' less these expenses is the 'operating income'.

- ➤ The restaurant's 'net income' is calculated by deducting the interest, depreciation, and income tax expenses from operating income.

Sales

Sales are divided into food, beverage and, if applicable, sundry categories. It is important for management to be able to track sales by major source of revenue. In addition, separating food, beverage and sundry sales allows for an accurate analysis of cost of sales for each category.

Food

All sales of food and non-alcoholic beverages are reported in this line item. Food sales are generally reported as one amount in the income statement but, where practical, it is helpful to maintain records for sales by area (e.g. restaurant, bar, take-out, delivery) in the books of account. This breakdown will allow management to analyze trends in sales for each area. In small restaurants this may not be necessary, or practical.

Beverage

Beverage sales include all sales of liquor, beer and wine. Generally, the total sales are reported on the income statement and a more detailed breakdown by category is contained in the books of account.

Sundry

Sundry sales include revenues for items other than food or beverage. Common examples of sundry sales include minimum order amounts, receipts from pay phones, vending machines and jukeboxes. Additionally, sundry sales include the sale of merchandise (e.g. T-shirts, sweatshirts) and retail products (e.g. candy, gum), excluding food.

In restaurants, nightclubs, bars or lounges where revenue generated from cover charges is significant, management may wish to report this revenue on a separate line item entitled, 'sales - entertainment'.

Sundry sales are also often referred to as 'other sales'. However, the term 'other' is frequently used to describe sub-categories (e.g. 'other cost of sales - food'). The use of the term 'sundry' will avoid unnecessary confusion.

Cost of sales

The cost of food and beverage sold in a period is based on the amount of inventory used. This amount is calculated either through a periodic or perpetual inventory system. The periodic inventory system requires less time to maintain, but provides less accurate operational information than the perpetual inventory system. Both are detailed in Chapter Three, Internal Controls. Management should examine both systems and determine which is best suited for their restaurant.

Whether inventory is accounted for on a perpetual or a periodic basis (see discussion under Inventory in the Balance Sheet section), it will affect the calculation of cost of sales. Under a perpetual inventory system, a running total of the inventory value is maintained in the books of account. Thus, the amount of inventory used is easy to calculate. Maintaining a perpetual inventory system is very time consuming if a restaurant has a large number of inventory items.

When inventory is accounted for on a periodic basis the cost of sales is calculated as follows:

Beginning inventory
+ Purchases
- Ending inventory
= Inventory used

Purchases are obtained from the trial balance and should include all purchases received during the month, including those purchases, which have not yet been paid for. The cost of food sold includes the purchase of:

➤ Produce, dairy products, meats, poultry, seafood, bread, dried and canned goods, non-alcoholic beverages (e.g. soft drinks, juices, milk) and miscellaneous food items.

The cost of beverage sold includes the purchase of:

➤ Liquor, wine, beer and other miscellaneous alcoholic beverage items.

Sundry costs are those costs associated directly with sundry sales. For example, if candy and sweatshirts are tracked as sundry sales, then the associated product costs are the sundry cost of sales.

It is necessary to separately count food, beverage and sundry inventory in order to be able to calculate and track each category's costs. These costs are then compared to their corresponding revenue (e.g. food cost is compared to food sales).

Total cost of sales

The total cost of sales is the total of food, beverage and sundry costs. These total costs are compared to total sales.

Gross margin

The gross margin is the portion of the revenue left after the total cost of sales has been deducted. Success for a restaurant often hinges on how well the gross margin is controlled. Thus, this sub-total requires careful monitoring by management.

Salaries, wages and benefits

The total cost of salaries and wages for all restaurant staff (hourly and salaried employees, and management) are included in this category. Also included are any bonuses paid, or payable. While the costs of salaries, wages and benefits are reported as one amount in the income statement, management may wish to separate salaries and wages from benefits in a separate schedule. This will allow management to monitor the relationship of benefits to salaries and wages.

Employee benefits include, but are not limited to, the following:

Mandatory benefits *(may vary by province):*

employer's portion of Canada Pension Plan (CPP);
employer's portion of Employment Insurance (EI);
Employer Health Tax (EHT);
Workers' Compensation (WC); and,
vacation pay.

Discretionary benefits:

employee meals;
employee social events;
income sharing; and,
other employee benefits.

In order to simplify record keeping, management may wish to coordinate the pay periods with the reporting periods. For instance if the restaurant reports on a four-week period, the employee's pay period should end on the last day of that period, regardless of when they are actually paid. If the reporting periods end on the last day of each month, management may consider having the pay periods end on the 15th and last day of the month. Both approaches will eliminate the need to accrue the salaries and wages that have been earned by, but not paid to, employees. It is important to note that under both approaches many employee benefits may still have to be accrued. For example, if a restaurant does not pay out vacation pay every cheque, but rather pays it only when the employee actually takes a vacation, then this benefit is being accrued. However, by having the pay periods correspond to the reporting periods, the amount of accrual accounting required should be reduced.

Occupancy

Occupancy expenses include:

➤ rent, both fixed and variable (e.g. percentage of gross sales);

➤ business and property taxes; and,

➤ property insurance.

Operating

Operating expenses are costs attributable directly to running the restaurant and include, but are not limited to, the following:

- costs of linen rentals and laundry;
- utilities (e.g. heating, lighting, power, gas, hydro);
- repairs and maintenance;
- equipment rentals;
- contract cleaning (e.g. night cleaners, window washing, carpet cleaning);
- bar supplies (e.g. swizzle sticks, bar napkins, straws, corkscrew);
- supplies (cleaning, paper, and guest supplies);
- automobile (e.g. car payments, insurance, repairs and maintenance, gas and oil);
- decorating (e.g. flowers, plants, centerpieces, display tables);
- printing and photocopying (e.g. menus and wine lists);
- incidental costs of replacing china, glassware, silverware, utensils, linens and uniforms (the original cost of these items are accounted for as property, plant and equipment); and,
- miscellaneous (costs directly related to the operation of the restaurant but not allocated to the above expense classifications).

General and administrative

General and administrative expenses include costs related to the general office, accounting, personnel, and credit card and collection activities. General and administrative expenses include the following:

- office supplies (e.g. paper, calculators, pens);
- photocopying and data processing;
- travel and entertainment;
- uncovered balances in the cash over(short) account;
- credit card commissions;
- dues, fees and licences;
- liability insurance (property insurance is an occupancy expense, while automobile insurance is an operating expense);
- professional fees (e.g. bookkeeper, accountant, lawyer, or consultant);
- security (security system or security personnel);
- telephone;

- capital taxes;
- bank charges; and,
- miscellaneous (e.g. costs of incorporation).

Marketing

Marketing covers all the expenses associated with promoting and marketing the restaurant, including:

- paid advertising;
- promotions;
- complimentary drinks or meals;
- market research;
- public relations; and,
- sponsorship.

Where significant amounts are spent on a specific marketing activity it is useful to track the associated expenses separately. Promotions that involve providing complimentary food and/or beverages should be broken down by food, liquor, beer and wine.

Entertainment

This category is necessary in restaurants, nightclubs, bars or lounges, where entertainment represents a significant expense. In restaurants where entertainment consists of simply providing music through a sound system, the cost of providing such music can be included in operating expenses. Entertainment expenses include:

- mechanical music;
- cost of hiring musicians/performers;
- booking agents' fees;
- transportation and accommodation for artists;
- equipment rentals;
- piano rental and tuning costs; and,
- costs of meals served to musicians/performers.

Royalty fees

While royalty fees are a type of marketing expense, they are usually of sufficient significance that they should be reported separately. Royalty fees include payment for continuing rights under a franchise agreement and for general or specific services provided by a franchisor. It is not necessary to include this line item on the income statement if the restaurant is not a franchise operation.

Operating income

Operating income summarizes the financial operating performance of the restaurant. This line item is a key figure in valuing the business and is generally used as a base for employee incentive and profit-sharing programs.

Operating income represents profit after all variable and fixed operating expenses. All subsequent deductions are non-operational expenses and include, for example:

> interest expense which relates to the financial structure of the restaurant (amount of debt);

> depreciation, which is a non-cash-flow item; and,

> income tax, which is paid after all operational expenses are deducted.

Non-operational expenses

Interest

The interest expense represents the costs associated with all outstanding short-term and long-term loans to the restaurant. The interest owed will be, for example:

> the interest on long-term debt used for the development of the restaurant;

> the interest on short-term debt (i.e. debt repaid within one year);

> the interest on an operating line of credit; and,

> the interest on any other cash loan used by the restaurant.

The interest expense related to long-term debt must be detailed separately either in the income statement or in the notes to the financial statements (Exhibit 6).

Depreciation and amortization

Depreciation is the method for writing down the cost of tangible assets or property, plant and equipment, while amortization is the method for writing down intangible assets (e.g. franchise fees). Depreciation and amortization charges do not represent cash outlays for the restaurant. Rather, they represent an allocation of the costs spent on purchasing an asset. For an explanation of how to calculate depreciation refer to the discussion on property, plant and equipment in the Balance Sheet section.

Income before income tax

In a sole proprietorship (one owner) or a partnership (two or more owners), income tax is levied on the proprietor or the partners, not on the restaurant itself. Therefore, for these types of business structures, income before income taxes is equal to net income.

If the business is incorporated, it is necessary to compute the income tax owing and deduct this amount in order to calculate net income.

Income tax

In general, income tax is only calculated at the restaurant's fiscal year end. If for internal purposes management wishes to report income taxes for each reporting period, an allocation of 18 percent (an estimate only) of income before income taxes may be used for earnings up to $500,000. It is important to note that when preparing financial statements under GAAP, certain expenses (e.g. amortization) may be recognized in different reporting periods for accounting and tax purposes. In such cases, income taxes to be paid for the year and income tax expense reported on the income statement will be different. This difference is recorded as 'future taxes' (i.e. a liability on the balance sheet). It is advisable to consult an accountant on all issues regarding taxes.

Net income

Net income is the residual balance after all of the above expenses have been deducted from the reporting period's sales.

Statement of Retained Earnings

The statement of retained earnings, illustrated in Exhibit 3, reports the changes in the restaurant's retained earnings during the reporting period. Retained earnings are the net accumulation of the restaurant's net income (loss) less dividends paid out.

The statement of retained earnings is the link between the balance sheet and the income statement.

Exhibit 3
Statement of Retained Earnings

SAMPLE RESTAURANT		
Statement Of Retained Earnings		
For the year ended December 31, 20x2		
	20x2	20x1
Retained Earnings, Beginning Period	$114,399	$47,656
Net Income	88,217	76,743
Dividend	(60,000)	(10,000)
Retained Earnings, End of Period	$142,616	$114,399
(see accompanying notes to financial statements)		

Format of statement of retained earnings

The statement of retained earnings is broken into the following categories:

Retained earnings, beginning of period

The first line of the statement reports the balance in the retained earnings account at the beginning of the reporting period, which is the balance at the end of the previous period.

Net income

The net income from the income statement is reported and added to the retained earnings, as illustrated.

Dividends

Dividends are an amount paid out of net income to shareholders as a return on their investment in the restaurant. The total amount of the dividends paid out during the period is reported and deducted from the retained earnings.

Retained earnings, end of period

The retained earnings, end of period is the sum of the retained earnings, beginning of period, plus the period's net income and less the dividends paid in the period.

The ending balance in retained earnings is then included in the balance sheet under the caption of shareholders' or owners' equity. This amount also becomes the 'retained earnings, beginning of period' for the next reporting period.

Balance Sheet

The balance sheet, illustrated in Exhibit 4, shows the financial position of the restaurant on the close of business of a particular date. Financial position is reported by listing the restaurant's assets, liabilities (debts), and the shareholders' (or owners') equity. If the restaurant is incorporated, the balance sheet will report shareholders' equity. If it is a sole proprietorship or a partnership, owners' equity will be reported. For the purpose of this section the restaurant will be assumed to be incorporated.

The assets on a balance sheet must equal the sum of the liabilities and the shareholders' equity. The reason for this is that one side (assets) reports the restaurant's resources while the other side (liabilities and shareholders' equity) reports how these resources were supplied.

- ➤ The assets of a restaurant are the economic resources owned by the restaurant. They include cash, amounts owed to the restaurant by its customers (called accounts receivable), inventories of food and beverage, prepaid expenses, deposits, property, plant and equipment, franchise fee and notes receivable.

- ➤ The liabilities of a restaurant are its debts and include amounts owed to suppliers, deposits received from customers, salaries and wages owed to employees, accrued expenses, taxes payable, bank loans payable, monies due to shareholders and notes payable.

- ➤ Shareholders' equity discloses the amount received attributable to capital for common and preferred shares issued and the restaurant's retained earnings. In addition, the number of common and preferred shares authorized and issued is reported. The retained earnings is made up of the cumulative net income (net loss) less the dividends paid out.

Exhibit 4
Balance Sheet

SAMPLE RESTAURANT
Balance Sheet
For the year ended December 31, 20x2

ASSETS	20x2	20x1	LIABILITIES	20x2	20x1
Current:			Current:		
Cash	$113,820	$59,811	Accounts Payable	$27,140	$29,480
Accounts Receivable	6,927	5,820	Deposits	10,500	15,000
Inventory (Note 1a)			Sales Tax & GST/HST	13,296	14,331
Food	9,843	10,597	Accrued Expenses	5,492	11,527
Beverage	10,269	9,869	Accrued Interest on Loan	2,000	9,200
other	7,322	7,553	Current Portion of		
Prepaid Expenses	5,444	5,835	Long Term Debt	135,275	157,775
Deposits	4,600	3,500	Payroll Liability	4,900	5,800
Total Current Assets	$168,225	$102,985	Total Current Liabilities	$198,603	$243,113
Fixed Assets (Note 2):			Long Term:		
Land	$100,000	$100,000	Bank Loan (Note 3)	$0	$0
Building	145,794	145,794	Due to Shareholders	10,000	10,000
Automobiles	88,921	88,921	Total Long Term Liabilities	$10,000	$10,000
Leasehold Improvements	156,450	156,450	Total Liabilities	$208,603	$253,113
Furniture, Fixtures & Equipment	445,084	445,084			
Less: Accumulated Depreciation	400,255	318,704	SHAREHOLDERS' EQUITY		
			Common shares		
Franchise Fee	0	0	Authorized – unlimited		
Notes Receivable	0	0	Issued - 12,000	$240,000	$240,000
Total Fixed Assets	$535,994	$617,545	Preferred Shares	113,000	113,000
			Authorized - unlimited		
			Issued - 11,300		
			cumulative		
Total Assets	$704,219	$720,530	Retained Earnings	142,616	114,399
			Total Shareholders' Equity:	$495,616	$467,399
			Total Liabilities AND Shareholders' Equity	$704,219	$720,512

(See accompanying Notes to Financial Statements)

A balance sheet should be prepared every time an income statement is prepared (e.g. every four weeks or month). The balance sheet provides an overview of the restaurant's financial liquidity and is a valuable management tool to have on a frequent basis. However, some managers feel that the restaurant's liquidity needs to be analyzed only every quarter and, therefore, prepare a balance sheet only four times a year.

The information to prepare the balance sheet is taken from the books of account which are discussed in Chapter Two. At the end of every reporting period, a trial balance is prepared which lists the balances for every account in the general ledger as at period end. These account balances are then allocated to their appropriate place in the financial statements. The chart of accounts in the Appendix provides a comprehensive list of all the accounts, organized by financial statement.

Format of balance sheet assets

As previously detailed, assets are the economic resources owned by the restaurant. The asset section of the balance sheet distinguishes between current and long-term assets. Current assets are those which are cash or are expected to be converted to cash within one year from the date of the balance sheet.

Long-term assets in restaurants consist primarily of property, plant and equipment (e.g. the building). These are assets which can be expected to be used by the restaurant for a period of longer than one year and are not highly liquid (cannot be easily converted to cash).

Current assets

Cash

For presentation purposes on the balance sheet, all the restaurant's bank accounts are grouped together and reported as one amount. In addition, any monies and/or receipts in the restaurant's safe are also included in this amount. For bookkeeping purposes a separate ledger account should be set up for each of the restaurant's bank accounts. The types of bank accounts a restaurant may have, include:

➤ An 'operating account' which is the primary bank account for the restaurant. Most cash disbursements (cheques) will be made from this account, and deposits of restaurant sales will be made to this account.

➤ A 'payroll account' should be established, particularly when a computerized payroll system is used. This account will usually have a nominal balance except on pay day when a transfer is made from the operating account to cover the period's payroll.

➤ A 'credit card account' may need to be opened if the credit card is aligned with a bank that requires its merchants to open an account in which to accumulate credit card receipts.

➤ A separate 'tax account' may be opened for accumulating provincial sales taxes (PST) , goods and services tax (GST) and harmonized sales tax (HST) collected on behalf of the government. The reason this type of account is recommended is that the restaurant is liable to the government for the PST and GST/HST collected. Therefore, it is important that there are sufficient funds to pay the government and that the money not be used to cover other operating expenses.

Accounts receivable

Trade receivables or customer receivables are not normally significant in restaurants as the majority of sales are paid by cash or credit card. Receivables in the balance sheet are presented net of any allowance for bad debts (i.e. customers that are unlikely to pay their debts).

Credit card sales that are directly deposited to the restaurant's bank account are reported as cash and not as accounts receivable. Credit card sales that are not 'direct deposited' and are outstanding at the date of the balance sheet are reported as accounts receivable.

Inventory

A restaurant's inventory is reported as a current asset and is generally broken down into three categories: food, beverage and other. The reason the categories are reported separately is to allow for the comparison of each category's inventory levels with sales, and to calculate the category's cost of sales.

Other inventory includes supplies of paper goods, linen, cutlery, china, cleaning supplies and other miscellaneous goods. These items may or may not be accounted for on an inventory basis depending on their value. If it is not a significant amount of money and the purchases occur relatively evenly throughout the year, the items can be expensed as they are purchased. This eliminates the need to take a physical count. However, if these expenses are high and the item's value high, then they should be counted and treated as an asset.

In a perpetual inventory system (in which inventory records are updated continuously) it is still necessary to perform periodic inventory counts. This will ensure that the system is operating effectively and that waste or theft is not occurring.

In a periodic inventory system, inventories are counted at the end of every reporting period in order to provide the information needed to calculate the cost of sales during the period (beginning inventory + purchases - ending inventory = cost of goods sold).

The most common method of valuing inventory in restaurants is the first-in, first-out (FIFO) method. However, the average cost method is also acceptable. Both methods are outlined below.

First-in, first-out (FIFO):

➤ This method assumes that the first goods purchased are the first used. Therefore, costs of sales are costed at the oldest unit cost and inventory is costed at the newer unit cost. A reasonable approximation of FIFO costing is to value all the inventory at the most recent invoice price.

Average cost:

➤ This method assumes that the average cost is the best way to value inventory and establish the cost of sales. Thus, an item is costed identically, regardless of whether it has been sold or remains in inventory. This method is more popular for computerized inventory systems where the calculation of average cost is performed by the computer.

Inventory items which are found to be spoiled or missing should be reported as a cost of sales in the period.

Prepaid expenses

Prepaid expenses are expenditures made for the benefit of future operations. For example, the insurance for the entire year is normally paid at the beginning of the year. If a balance sheet is prepared before the end of the year it is necessary to calculate the amount of insurance for the remaining months of the year. This amount is reported as a prepaid expense.

In order to track expenditures (e.g. insurance, rent), prepaid expenses may be recorded in separate accounts in the books of account. However, only the total amount is reported on the balance sheet.

Deposits

Deposits paid by the restaurant (e.g. deposits held by utility companies as security against future expenditures) may be recorded in separate accounts in the chart of accounts. In the balance sheet only the total amount of deposits are reported.

Property, plant and equipment

Property, plant and equipment include:

➤ land;

➤ building(s);

➤ furniture, fixtures and equipment;

➤ leasehold improvements; and,

➤ automobile(s).

These assets are used to produce revenue over a period of years, and accordingly, their costs are depreciated (reduced) over their useful lives in order to match the costs with the related revenues.

The chart of accounts has separate accounts for each category of asset. The assets are recorded at cost in these accounts and a corresponding account should be set up to record the amount of accumulated depreciation for each asset. The amount to be depreciated is the fixed asset's original cost less any salvage or residual value. The balance sheet should report each asset's purchase price and the total accumulated depreciation for all the assets. The breakdown of gross costs and accumulated depreciation should be detailed in a note to the financial statements. In preparing the balance sheet (Exhibit 4) the assets were depreciated using the sample rates and methods detailed below. It is advisable to seek an accountant's advice as to how the capital assets should be depreciated over their useful lives.

➤ Land is assumed to have unlimited life and, therefore, is not depreciated.

➤ Buildings can be depreciated under several accounting methods. The most prevalent practice in the restaurant industry is to use the declining balance method at five percent per year. Using this method, a set percentage of the net value of the asset (cost less accumulated depreciation) is depreciated each year.

➤ Furniture, fixtures and equipment are normally depreciated using the declining balance method at 20 percent per year.

➤ Leasehold improvements are improvements made to the leased space by the lessee and are depreciated over the existing term of the lease plus one renewable term. Leasehold improvements include, but are not limited to, the cost of building partitions, installing additional plumbing, installing electrical wiring, building counters, installing flooring, and painting the walls.

➤ Operating equipment includes such items as linens, stemware, cutlery, china and utensils. The useful life of these items is normally much shorter than that of the other property, plant and equipment and, thus, they are depreciated at a much faster rate. Normally 50 percent of the purchases of operating equipment are written off in the year acquired, and the remaining 50 percent are written off in the following year. This rate of amortization is much faster than the general amortization for furniture, fixtures and equipment as operating equipment usually has an extremely short life due to breakage and wear and tear and, therefore, needs a fast amortization. Incidental amounts spent to replace broken or missing items are usually written off as operating expenses when they occur.

➤ Automobiles are depreciated on a declining balance basis at 30 percent per year. However, for income tax purposes, consultation with an accountant is advisable.

It is possible that the depreciation policies applied to the capital assets may be consistent with the method used when calculating depreciation for income tax purposes (capital cost allowance). Management should seek an accountant's opinion as to which depreciation policies and capital cost allowances to use. If the estimated future net cash flows from use of a fixed asset (including any salvage or residual values) fall below the depreciated amount at which the asset is being carried, a write down is necessary. The excess of the fixed asset's carrying amount over the estimated future net cash flows would be charged as an expense.

Capital leases

An asset leased by a restaurant is reported as a capital lease when the lessor transfers substantially the benefits and risks of ownership to the lessee (e.g. restaurant). This 'substantial transfer' occurs when one or more of the following conditions exist at the beginning of the lease:

> ➤ Reasonable assurance that the restaurant will obtain ownership of the leased property by the end of the lease term;

> ➤ Lessee will receive substantially all of the economic benefits expected to be derived from the leased property over its life span; and/or,

> ➤ Lessor will recover his/her investment in the leased property and a return on investment as a result of the lease agreement.

Assets reported as capital leases are reported separately from other assets owned by the restaurant. In addition, obligations related to capital leases are reported separately from other long-term obligations. Management should seek an accountant's opinion as to how to account for capital leases.

For all leases, capital and operating, the future minimum lease payments in total and for each of the next five years should be disclosed in the notes to the financial statements (see Exhibit 6).

Franchise fee

Franchise agreements often require that an initial franchise fee be paid and that a certain amount be spent on leasehold improvements in order to meet the standards required by the franchisor. This initial fee may cover the cost for the initial services provided by the franchisor including, but not limited to: assistance in selecting a location, obtaining financing, designing the restaurant, advertising, personnel training, setting up books of account, and implementing quality control systems.

The amount paid as a franchise fee is an asset and should be amortized over the term of the franchise agreement. The amounts spent on inventory and leasehold improvements should be recorded as inventory and leasehold improvements and not as franchise fees.

Notes receivable

Notes receivable report the loans made by the restaurant to its shareholders and/or others.

Goodwill

Goodwill is reported on a company's, or individual's, financial statements to account for the difference between the purchase price of, for example, a restaurant and the current fair market value of the acquired assets. Goodwill is carried in the balance sheet without reference to any amortization term. It is now recognized as an intangible asset with an infinite life. Management, however, needs to apply an impairment test at least once annually. Where the impairment is considered permanent in nature, a full charge is to be booked in income. This is a complex area and management should seek professional advice when assessing goodwill.

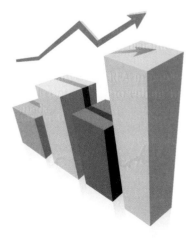

Liabilities and shareholder equity

Liabilities represent the debts owed to the creditors of the restaurant. Shareholders' equity represents the shareholders' interest in the assets of the restaurant.

In a manner that is similar to the asset side of the balance sheet, liabilities are divided between current and long-term. Current liabilities are liabilities that will be paid within one year of the date of the balance sheet, unless contractual arrangements have been made for settlement from other than current assets. For example, when a bank loan is due within the year, but contractual arrangements have been made for refinancing the loan.

Long-term liabilities are those amounts owed to creditors that are not required to be paid within one year of the date of the balance sheet.

Current liabilities

The following make up current liabilities.

Accounts payable

Accounts payable include all invoices for goods or services received, but not paid, at the date of the balance sheet.

Trade accounts with food and beverage suppliers will likely represent the majority of this account.

Deposits

The restaurant may have deposits on hand that are collected from customers for services that are to be held in the future (e.g. banquet, party). In this case the deposit is included in liabilities until the event occurs and then the amount can be considered earned by the restaurant.

Sales tax and GST/HST

Significant current liabilities for restaurants are provincial sales tax (PST) , the federal goods and services tax (GST) or harmonized sales tax (HST) collected from customers but not yet remitted to the government.

All PST collected from customers and the net amount of the GST or HST payable to the government is reported in this account. The net GST/HST is the difference between the GST/HST collected from customers and the GST/HST paid by the restaurant to its suppliers.

Payroll liabilities

Payroll liabilities include all salaries, wages and benefits incurred but not paid, including the employer's and employees' contribution to Canada Pension Plan, Employment Insurance, Employer Health Tax, workers' compensation, vacation pay, and withheld income tax (both accrued and payable).

Accrued expenses

Accrued expenses are expenses that have been incurred but have not been paid. In this situation, it will be necessary to estimate these expenses in order to ensure that all costs related to the reported revenue are included on the income statement. An example of accrued expenses is the interest on a bank loan if the date that the interest is payable differs from the balance sheet date.

A restaurant can, if management wishes, report income tax payable as a separate line item under current liabilities.

Current portion of long-term debt

This line item reports the portion of any long-term debt (principal payments) which is payable within one year of the balance sheet date.

Long-term liabilities

The following make up long-term liabilities:

Bank loan and other indebtedness

The amount of any notes payable, bank loans or bonds would be included. This amount is shown net of the current portion of the debt which is reported in current liabilities. However, if the bank loan is a 'demand loan', it must be carried 100% as a short-term liability, as the bank can call the loan at any time.

Due to shareholders

Long-term debt due to shareholders is reported separately from amounts due to parties that do not have an ownership interest in the restaurant.

Shareholders' or owner's equity

Shareholders' equity represents the shareholders' interest in the assets of the restaurant. For restaurants that are incorporated, the balance sheet will report shareholders' equity. Restaurants that are sole proprietorships or partnerships will report owner's equity.

Shareholders' equity

When the business is incorporated, the shareholders' equity should:

- ➤ Report the amounts received attributable to capital for both common and preferred shares.

- ➤ Disclose the number of common and preferred shares issued and authorized. If there is more than one class of either common or preferred shares, they should be shown separately.

- ➤ The retained earnings, end of period are included in shareholders' equity. This account includes all net income (or net losses) from inception of the business, less all dividends paid out to shareholders.

Owner's equity

If the business is not incorporated, an owner's equity account should be presented for each individual with an ownership stake in the business. This account should report the amount invested by the owner, plus the owner's share of all net income (or net losses) from inception of the business, less all financial drawings taken by the owner.

Loans to or from the business are not included in this account, but are included under liabilities and assets, respectively.

Statement of Cash Flow

The statement of cash flow, illustrated in Exhibit 5, reports where the restaurant's funds came from and what they were spent on, during the period. This statement is a useful complement to the balance sheet and income statement since it highlights the flow of cash in and out of the restaurant, and shows the restaurant's ability to meet its current financial obligations. The statement enables shareholders to monitor the restaurant's ability to pay dividends and to meet its credit obligations.

The statement of cash flow does not have to be prepared as frequently as an income statement but can be prepared every quarter. In the short term (four week period) management should have a good understanding of the restaurant's cash flow position. However, in the medium term (three months) and long term (year) management should have updated reports which will help them monitor and manage the restaurant's funds. The statement of cash flow must be prepared at the fiscal year end.

The information to prepare the statement of cash flow comes from the books of account which are discussed in Chapter Two. At the end of every period a trial balance should be prepared which lists the period end balances in every account. These account balances are then allocated to their appropriate place in the financial statements.

Format of the statement of cash flow

The statement of cash flow reports the changes in cash position that are the result of the restaurant's activities during the period. The restaurant's activities are reported under the following headings:

➤ Operating Activities;

➤ Investing Activities; and,

➤ Financing Activities.

Exhibit 5

37

Statement of Cash Flow

SAMPLE RESTAURANT Statement of Cash Flow For the year ended December 31, 20x2	20x2	20x1
Cash Provided by (used in) Operating Activities		
Net Income	$88,217	$76,743
Add: Changes to operations not requiring a current payment:		
Depreciation & Amortization	81,551	98,428
Net Change in non-cash Working Capital	-25,759	-21,085
Cash Provided by Operating Activities	$144,009	$154,086
Cash Provided by (used in) Investing Activities		
Purchase of Furniture & Fixtures	0	-85,580
Cash used in Investing Activities	0	-85,580
Cash Provided by (used in) Financing Activities		
Repayment of Bank Loan	-20,000	-10,000
Dividends	-60,000	-10,000
Cash used Financing Activities	-80,000	-20,000
Net Increase in Cash During the Year	64,009	48,506
Cash Beginning of Year	59,881	11,305
Cash End of Year	$123,890	$59,811
(See accompanying Notes to Financial Statements)		

Operating activities

Operating activities report the restaurant's cash flow for the period. The base for calculating this cash flow is the net income, which is adjusted to reflect the reporting of non-cash expenses on the income statement. For example, depreciation is deducted from sales on the income statement. However, depreciation does not reflect an actual cash expenditure. Therefore, depreciation charges are added back in this section of the statement of cash flow.

Also included in operating activities is the net change in non-cash working capital during the period. This amount reflects the net change in current assets (other than cash) and current liabilities. For example, an increase in accounts payable is a source of cash while an increase in inventory represent a use of cash. To calculate the net change in non-cash working capital management should:

➤ List all of last period's working capital items (current assets and current liabilities), excluding cash, in one column and this period's corresponding working capital items in the next column.

➤ Calculate the difference between the columns.

– An increase in any current asset represents a use of cash in the period, while a decrease represents a source of cash.

– An increase in any current liability represents a source of cash in the period, while a decrease represents a use of cash.

➤ Report the net amount as the 'net change in non-cash working capital during the period'.

Investing activities

Investing activities are transactions the restaurant enters into, such as investments or acquisition of property, plant and equipment. For example, the down payment on the purchase of a building is a decrease in cash flow resulting from investing activities.

Therefore, investing activities are additions and disposals of non-current assets and are listed by category of asset.

Financing activities

Changes in capital invested in the business from either the creditors or the share-holders are reported as changes in financing activities. For example, the amount of a new bank loan in the period is an increase in cash flow from financing activities.

For purposes of comparability between restaurants, dividends should be included as a financing activity. There are arguments supporting the inclusion of dividends as either an operating activity or a financing activity. However, for the purpose of uniformity throughout the restaurant industry, it is best to report dividends as a financing activity.

Net changes in cash

The sum of cash provided (used) in operating, investing and financing activities is added to the opening period's cash balance. This total is the amount of cash at the end of the period and is reported as the cash balance on the balance sheet.

Notes to the Financial Statements

A t the back of the financial statements there are usually several notes which detail the relevant accounting policies followed in preparing the statements. In addition, the notes to the financial statements contain information that does not appear elsewhere in the financial statements but that must be provided in order to comply with Canadian GAAP. Examples of notes to the financial statements are illustrated in Exhibit 6.

What information to include

Generally the following information is provided in the notes to the financial statements:

- ➤ Description of the significant accounting policies (e.g. the method of valuing inventory, the method of depreciating property, plant and equipment).

- ➤ Disclosure where assets are pledged as security against liabilities.

- ➤ Schedule of property, plant and equipment, by class, listing gross cost, accumulated depreciation, and net book value (must agree with the amount presented on the balance sheet).

- ➤ Disclosure of any contingencies (e.g. guarantees).

- ➤ Disclosure of the details of any long-term debt, including the interest rate and the expected annual repayments for the next five years.

- ➤ Disclosure of any commitments (e.g. lease agreements).

- ➤ Explanation of any changes in shareholders' equity (e.g. new shares issued, stock splits).

- ➤ Disclosure of significant characteristics of the different classes of share capital (e.g. dividend rates on preferred shares and whether or not they are cumulative; the existence of conversion provisions).

- ➤ The amount of any loss carry forwards for income tax purposes, including their expiry date, if applicable.

Exhibit 6

41

Chapter One

Notes to the Financial Statements

1. Significant Accounting Policies

The accounting policies of the company are in accordance with the generally accepted accounting principles. The following is a summary of the significant accounting policies followed in the preparation of these financial statements.

a. Inventories
    Inventories are priced at the lower cost or market value with cost being determined on a first-out basis.
b. Property, plant and equipment
    Property, plant and equipment are recorded at cost with depreciation being provided at the following annual rates:

Leasehold improvements	Straight line over 10 years
Furniture, fixtures & equipment	Declining balance at 20 percent
Building	Declining balance at 5 percent
Automobile	Declining balance at 30 percent

Operating equipment is recorded at cost and depreciated on a straight line basis over 2 years. The company's operating equipment is now fully depreciated and is not included in the financial statements. Incidental purchases of operating equipment are expensed as incurred.

2. Property, plant and equipment

The major categories of property, plant and equipment are:

	Original Cost	Accumulated Depreciation	Net Book Value	Previous Net Book Value
Leasehold Improvements	$156,450	$62,580	$93,870	$109,515
Furniture, fixtures & equipment	445,084	243,060	202,024	252,530
Building	145,794	27,044	118,750	125,000
Automobile	88,921	67,571	21,350	30,500
Total	$836,249	$400,255	$435,994	$517,545

3. Bank Loan

The bank loan of $135,276 bears interest at prime plus 1 3/4 percent per annum and is secured by all the assets of the company and personal guarantees of the shareholders. In the year 20x2, the restaurant's 4th operating year, the company retired $20,000 of long-term debt. (It is common and prudent in the restaurant industry to retire all debt within three to five years of start up) Short-term funds are borrowed at prime plus 2 percent. (Bank loans and short-term indebtedness represent debt and interest which must be repaid within one year.)

Scheduled repayments over the next five years are as follows:

20x3	$10,000
20x4	$10,000
20x5	$10,000
20x6	$10,000
20x7	$10,000

Financial Projections

As discussed earlier in this chapter, financial statements are a tool that management can use to evaluate the restaurant's historical performance and identify potential problems in the operation (e.g. high food cost). Financial projections are a valuable management tool as they provide a quantitative basis for making management decisions and serve as a budget for the restaurant's financial performance in the upcoming periods.

Projections should be realistic and provide financial benchmarks that the restaurant can achieve. For example, at the end of every reporting period, management should compare actual results with projections, and understand the reason for any variances. Based on this understanding, management can take actions to rectify any problems that may exist.

Management should prepare a 'projected income statement' for the upcoming fiscal year by four-week period, or month. There are two benefits to doing this breakdown:

> An in-depth analysis of each period's sales and expenses should result in a more accurate and realistic projection of the fiscal year's results.

> Management will be able to analyze actual results with projected results for the same period.

Projecting sales

The most difficult aspect of preparing projections is to accurately forecast sales for a period. In forecasting sales, management should take into account the following factors:

Historical sales by specific period

In projecting sales for a specific period, it is essential that management analyze the sales for the same period in the previous years. This analysis should include a breakdown of revenue by, for example:

> Meal period;

> average check; and,

> number of covers served.

In addition, management should identify any unusual events or activities that may have impacted sales (e.g. an advertising campaign) during the period.

Trends in sales over the last year(s)

The next step is to examine the trends in sales during the preceding periods. Management should then determine the reason for this trend (e.g. introduction of new promotions) and determine how this trend will impact future periods.

Operational changes that may impact sales

Management should identify any operational changes that have been implemented over the course of the last 12 months and determine what impact, if any, they have had on the restaurant's sales. In addition, management should take into account any operational changes that are proposed and/or planned for the projection period. Examples of operational changes include:

➤ Changes to the menu, either in items or pricing (may impact number of covers served, average check).

➤ Increase/decrease in seating capacity (may impact volume of business).

➤ Changes in production activity at the restaurant (which could impact labour costs)

➤ Changes in the level of service (e.g. if the restaurant is now providing full service where it was providing counter service)

Specific marketing activities

In projecting sales for the period, management should identify any marketing activities (e.g. promotions, advertising campaign, distribution of coupons) or media coverage (e.g. a restaurant review) that are being planned for those periods. These activities will likely impact the period's sales.

Prior to preparing financial projections, a marketing plan for the restaurant needs to be developed. While the marketing plan does not have to be very formal or lengthy, it does need to be thought out and documented. The marketing plan should identify the different activities that are being planned and, for each activity, an objective(s) should be set. The objective should be both qualitative (e.g. increase repeat business) and quantitative (e.g. increase the number of covers served by five percent).

Changes in the local market that may affect the restaurant

Management should monitor events and developments in the local market in order to take advantage of potential opportunities or mitigate the damage from other developments. Some examples include:

➤ The opening or closing of a competitive restaurant.

➤ The opening of a condominium or apartment building in the area.

➤ The opening of an office complex in the area.

➤ The staging of a special event in the local market (e.g. a festival) or the opening of a social venue (e.g. theatre, mall) in the vicinity of the restaurant.

Projecting expenses

For the purposes of preparing financial projections, management should determine which expenses are variable (expenses which vary with volume of sales) and which are fixed (expenses which remain relatively constant irrespective of sales).

When projecting variable expenses management should be concerned with operating ratios (percentage of gross sales) as opposed to dollar amounts. In projecting fixed expenses, management should recognize that certain expenses will remain constant throughout the year (a fixed lease) and others will vary by season (heating).

In projecting expenses, management should take into account the following factors:

Historical expenses by specific period

In projecting expenses for a specific period, it is essential that management analyze the expenses for the same period in the previous years. Management should also identify any unusual events or activities that may have impacted expenses (e.g. food cost was high because the refrigerator broke down and the food spoiled).

Trends in expenses over the last year(s)

The next step in preparing projections is to examine the trends in expenses during the preceding periods. Management should then determine the reason for this trend (e.g. implementation of internal controls) and determine how this trend will impact future periods.

Operational changes that may impact expenses

Management should identify any operational changes that have been implemented over the course of the last 12 months and determine what impact, if any, they have had, or will have, on the restaurant's expenses. In addition, management must take into account any operational changes that are proposed and/or planned for the projection period. In addition to the implementation of internal controls, examples of operational changes include:

- change in the terms of the lease;
- the launch of an advertising campaign;
- changes to the menu, either in items or pricing (may impact food cost);
- increase or decrease in seating capacity (may impact labour costs).

In preparing the financial projections, management should clearly document the assumptions that underlie the projections. These assumptions should be periodically reviewed to ensure that they are still valid. If the assumptions are no longer valid, the projections should be modified to reflect the new circumstances.

Ratio Analysis

Ratio analysis converts the dollar figures reported on the financial statements to percentages or ratios, and is an integral part of analyzing and understanding the statements. A ratio analysis examines the relationship between various items reported in the financial statements and allows for comparison between reporting periods and between restaurants.

There are six major types of ratios which are used to measure and evaluate a restaurant's overall performance:

➤ liquidity ratios;

➤ asset management ratios;

➤ debt management ratios;

➤ profitability ratios;

➤ value ratios; and,

➤ key operating ratios.

A discussion and example of each of these ratios follow.

Liquidity ratios

Liquidity ratios are used to analyze the ability of the restaurant to cover its short-term debt (debt to be paid within one year) with its operational cash flow. The only way to know if a restaurant can cover its short-term debt is by ensuring there are sufficient current assets to cover the debt. The best liquidity ratio to use in the restaurant business is the current ratio.

Current ratio

The current ratio is the most common measure to determine the restaurant's ability to pay off its current liabilities. The current ratio is calculated as follows:

$$\text{current ratio} = \frac{\text{current assets}}{\text{current liabilities}} = \frac{\$168,225}{\$135,275} = 1.24$$

Too low a ratio may indicate a difficulty to cover short-term debt. Too high a ratio may indicate having too much money tied up in current assets and which is not earning income. A ratio of 1 to 1 is appropriate for most restaurants.

Asset management ratios

Asset management ratios are designed to measure management's ability to effectively use the restaurant's assets. Asset management ratios will enable management to determine if the restaurant's assets are too high or too low. In restaurants, management must carefully monitor all assets, especially inventory.

Inventory utilization ratio

The inventory utilization ratio represents the average number of times inventory turns over during the reporting period. The ratio does not reflect how fast particular items are moving, but rather how fast all items on average are moving. Inventory turnover is directly related to the ability of management to control and effectively utilize the restaurant's inventory.

The number of times inventory turns over in a period is calculated as follows:

$$\text{inventory utilization} = \frac{\text{sales for period}}{\text{inventory}}$$

For example,

$$\frac{\text{beverage sales}}{\text{beverage inventory}} = \frac{\$304,482}{\$10,269} = 29.7 \text{ times}$$

Food inventory in a restaurant should turn over approximately 36 to 42 times in a year, which is approximately three to four times a month. Beverage inventory should turn over approximately two to two-and-a-half times in a month, or 24 to 30 times per year.

Debt management ratios

Debt management ratios measure the restaurant's financial leveraging. While high leverage positions are desirable in many businesses this is not true for restaurants. As the amount of debt increases, the shareholders' risk is reduced and the risk is placed onto the bank. However, bankers are averse to lending large amounts of unsecured capital to a restaurant and will insist on very secure collateral. Additionally, due to the potential short life of restaurants, debt and equity paybacks should be very quick (three to four years or 25 percent to 33 percent).

Debt ratio

The debt ratio measures total debt to total assets. This ratio measures the percentage of total funds provided by creditors. Creditors look for a low ratio to minimize their risks while operators look for a high ratio in order to increase their earnings on investment. The debt ratio is calculated as follows:

$$\text{debt ratio} = \frac{\text{total debt}}{\text{total assets}} = \frac{\$208,603}{\$704,219} = 29.6\%$$

A restaurant should carry a debt ratio of no higher than 50 percent, meaning that creditors should supply a maximum of 50 percent of the restaurant's total financing.

Profitability ratios

The profitability ratios analyze the restaurant's financial performance by assessing various income levels as a percentage of sales.

Operating income margin on sales

Operating income margin should be used to analyze the restaurant's financial operating performance relative to previous periods and industry averages. The operating income margin is the best measure of the operational performance of the restaurant. The operating income margin on sales is calculated as follows:

operating income margin on sales =

$$\frac{\text{operating income}}{\text{total sales}} = \frac{\$209,724}{\$1,611,016} = 13.0\%$$

A healthy ratio would be in the range of 10 percent to 15 percent.

Net income margin on sales

If the restaurant's net income margin on sales is below industry averages it will indicate to management that:

➤ the restaurant's volume of business or prices are too low;

➤ inventory and assets are not managed effectively; and/or,

➤ the restaurant has incurred too high of a debt load.

The net income margin is calculated as follows:

$$\text{net income margin} = \frac{\text{net income}}{\text{total sales}} = \frac{\$88,217}{\$1,611,016} = 5.5\%$$

A restaurant should aim for a net income margin of five percent or greater.

Value ratios

The value ratios are used to value the restaurant and to determine how the investors are doing with their investments. The most common value ratio is the return on investment (ROI) and is described below.

Return on investment

The return on investment allows the shareholders to assess the return they are receiving on their investment. There are several ways to calculate the return on investment, but generally it is calculated as follows:

$$\frac{\text{net income}}{\text{shareholders' equity}} = \frac{\$88,217}{\$495,616} = 17.8\%$$

Assessing the return on investment is a matter of personal opinion. Generally the investor should hope to earn a return that exceeds the return that would be earned on a secure long-term deposit.

Key operating ratios

The following key operating ratios are not considered financial ratios. However, they are a valuable tool for assessing the restaurant's financial performance. These ratios include:

Food, beverage and sundry ratios

Food, beverage and sundry ratios are used to analyze the restaurant's cost of sales. While there are no ideal ratios it is important for management to standardize costs (outlined in Chapter Three), and determine a theoretical cost for each area.

The percentages for the sample restaurant are:

$$\text{food percentage} = \frac{\text{food cost}}{\text{food sales}} = \frac{\$421,764}{\$1,240,482} = 34.0\%$$

$$\text{beverage percentage} = \frac{\text{beverage cost}}{\text{beverage sales}} = \frac{\$109,005}{\$304,482} = 35.8\%$$

$$\text{sundry percentage} = \frac{\text{sundry cost}}{\text{sundry sales}} = \frac{\$29,856}{\$66,052} = 45.2\%$$

The rules of thumb are that food cost should range from 22 percent to 40 percent, beverage costs should range from 25 percent to 40 percent, and sundry costs should be less than 100 percent.

Labour costs

Salary, wage and benefit costs are analyzed as a percentage of total sales and are calculated as follows:

labour cost =

$$\frac{\text{salaries, wages \& benefits}}{\text{total sales}} = \frac{\$512,303}{\$1,611,016} = 31.8\%$$

Ideally, restaurants should keep labour costs, including all benefits, under 32 percent.

Chapter Two

Basic Books of Account

The basic books of account outlined in this chapter are considered the framework for tracking all revenues and expenses in order to develop the financial statements detailed in Chapter One.

In essence, this section outlines good bookkeeping practices and provides forms, ledgers and journals which will assist in tracking financial transactions. A book-keeper should be able to easily follow this framework and produce statements which are easy to use and understand.

Management, in turn, should be able to read the financial statements and track historical data, as a clear understanding of the restaurant's financial position is necessary to operate effectively. The discussion on the books of account provides management with an understanding of how revenues and expenses are tracked throughout a reporting period.

Books of account provide the information required to:

➤   control cash flow;

➤   prepare financial statements;

➤   prepare operating statements;

➤   support the annual income tax return;

➤   support preparation of employees' T4s;

➤   properly remit the appropriate amount of provincial sales tax (PST) , goods and services tax (GST) or harmonized sales tax (HST) each month;

➤   support payment for goods and services received in case of a dispute; and,

➤   properly remit the appropriate employee and employer withholdings every month.

Books of account

The purpose of accounting is to accumulate information about all of a restaurant's financial transactions, in an organized manner, so that similar transactions are grouped together.

The basic flow of information in an accounting process is the following:

➤ All transactions (e.g. sales, wages, purchase of food) are recorded chronologically in the appropriate journal or sub-ledger. All transactions must be recorded as a double entry (there must be a debit and credit for every financial transaction).

➤ At the end of the reporting period, each journal and sub-ledger is totalled and these amounts are added to the appropriate ledger accounts in the general ledger. The purpose of the general ledger is to group transactions according to the account groupings detailed in the chart of accounts.

➤ After the general ledger has been updated a list of the accounts and their balance is prepared. This list is called the trial balance and is used as the basis for preparing the period's financial statements.

Exhibit 7 illustrates the accounting process for a restaurant in a flow-chart format. The flow chart shows how the daily transactions are tracked and ultimately reported in the financial statements.

The restaurant business has four main types of transactions and each has a distinct accounting system. The four transaction types are:

➤ Sales, receivables and cash system (sales in exchange for cash or receivables);

➤ purchase, payable and payments system (purchases in exchange for payables or cash);

➤ payroll system (salaries, wages and benefits paid to employees); and,

➤ inventory system (movements of items in and out of inventory).

Exhibit 7
Accounting Flow Chart

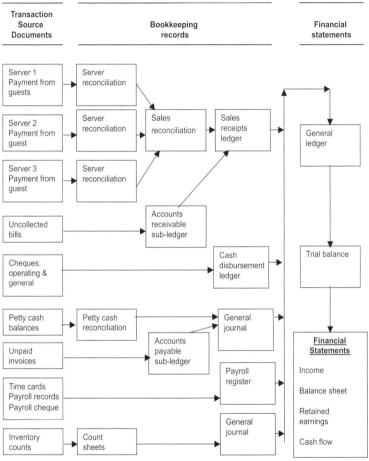

Automation

An important decision for management is whether to computerize the books of account. A manual accounting system will, like a computerized system, allocate transactions to the appropriate sub-ledger or journal. The totals are then carried forward to the general ledger, and finally to the financial statements. Having a computerized system does not eliminate the need to understand how the books of account system works, nor does it eliminate the need to ensure that all transactions are recorded. Therefore, the books of account are an integral part of the transaction reporting process in both a manual and computerized system and should be clearly understood by management.

The primary advantage of a computerized system is a reduction in the time required to input and compute the various statements. The decision on whether or not to computerize the books of account will depend primarily on two factors:

➤ The restaurant's volume of business:

The greater the number of transactions, the more sense it makes to consider computerizing. The computer processes transactions very quickly and can create significant time savings.

➤ The number of accounts in the chart of accounts:

The more detailed the chart of accounts, the more sense it makes to consider computerizing. A computer can track a greater number of accounts easily, making it possible to separately track, for example, food sales in the dining room, the lounge, and via take-out and delivery.

An added benefit of computerized systems is that they can be designed to accommodate the restaurant's system of internal controls. Internal controls are the management systems used to monitor the restaurant's prime costs (prime costs are defined as the cost of food, beverage and labour costs) on a daily basis, and are detailed in Chapter Three.

Many cash registers are small computers, capable of producing a summary report of transactions processed. These transaction reports can greatly simplify the system for reporting sales, receivables and cash.

Before purchasing a computer or software package (be it a cash register or a complete accounting and internal control system) it is important to ensure that the system will meet the restaurant's present and future needs. This should involve a careful review of the available technology at the time of purchase and discussions with other users.

As outlined earlier, the books of account are based on setting up accounting systems for four major transaction types:

➤   Sales, receivables and cash;

➤   purchases, payables, and payments;

➤   payroll; and,

➤   inventory.

The accounting systems described in this chapter apply to both a manual and computerized system and vary only in the mode of preparation. The resulting financial statements, detailed in Chapter One, will be the same.

Sales, Receivables and Cash

The sales, receivables and cash accounting system tracks food, beverage, and sundry sales. Sundry sales include, for example:

➤ cover charges;

➤ delivery charges;

➤ parking;

➤ valet;

➤ telephone;

➤ vending machine receipts; and,

➤ merchandise sales.

This system ensures that for the purposes of recording and collection, all of the following information is recorded:

➤ sales;

➤ cash available for deposit; and,

➤ receivables.

For most restaurants this accounting system begins with the servers. In many restaurants, servers act as their own cash bank in that they perform the following functions:

➤ handle a float;

➤ record their own sales;

➤ balance with cash register's summary report; and,

➤ make a daily deposit.

Server reconciliation

At the end of a shift each server should prepare a server reconciliation, illustrated in Exhibit 8.

Exhibit 8

Server Reconciliation Form

Name _____   Date _____   Section _____

Average Check _____   Voids _____   Shift _____

Number of guests _____

Reading (Total Sales) $ _____
VISA
MasterCard
American Express
House Charge
Other

Total Charges $ _____

Cash Owed $ _____
_____ x Coins   = _____
_____ x Loonies   = _____
_____ x Toonies   = _____
_____ x $5.00   = _____
_____ x $10.00   = _____
_____ x $20.00   = _____
_____ x $50.00   = _____
_____ x $100.00   = _____
_____ x Cheques   = _____

Total Cash & Cheques $ _____

Total Deposit to House (should equal Reading) $ _____

Variance $ _____

Server Signature _____   Manager Signature _____

The server reconciliation includes the name of the server, the date, the section number, average check, voids, number of guests served and the shift period.

The purpose of the server reconciliation is to ensure that the server remits cash and credit receipts that equal the total sales earned that shift. Any variance should be followed up and explained.

The average check (total sales divided by the number of customers served) is recorded at the top of the form. The average check is a useful basis for evaluating a server's performance. If one server consistently has an average check that is lower than the other servers, it may indicate a problem of theft or poor selling techniques.

A void occurs when a server enters an order, then backs out the order. This gives the server the opportunity to order an item(s) and then void the item(s) in order to avoid paying for it. Accordingly, it is important to keep records of servers' voids. The total dollar value of a server's voids is recorded on the 'Voids' line of the form.

The average check is recorded in order to analyze each server's sales ability and activity, while the number of guests illustrates how many guests a server handles per shift. The average check and number of guests served can be used to analyze server productivity on an individual or comparative basis.

In order to reconcile cash and credit card receipts the server should:

- ➤ Take the total sales reading from the cash register summary tape and enter the amount on the 'Reading' line.

- ➤ Enter the total receipts for each credit card type on the 'VISA', 'MasterCard', or 'American Express' lines.

- ➤ Enter the total house charges on the 'House Charge' line.

- ➤ Enter the total other receipts (e.g. other credit cards) on the 'Other' line.

- ➤ Write the total of these non-cash receipts on the 'Total Charges' Line.

- ➤ Calculate the 'Cash Owed' amount by subtracting the 'Total Charges' from the 'Reading' (Total Sales) figure.

- ➤ Enter the breakdown of the cash deposit by filling in the total cash to be deposited by denomination (including cheques) on the appropriate lines.

- ➤ Enter the total cash deposit (including cheques) in the 'Total Cash & Cheques' line.

- ➤ Write the sum of the 'Total Charges' amount and the cash deposit (including cheques) in the 'Total Deposit to the House' line.

- ➤ The difference between the 'Reading' and the 'Total Deposit to House' is entered in the 'Variance' line.

Once completed the server should sign the form indicating that the amounts are correct and give the form and deposit to the manager. The manager should verify the accuracy of the information and count the cash and receipts submitted. If the form and the deposit are correct, the manager signs the form and becomes responsible for the deposit and receipts.

Sales reconciliation

At the end of a shift, the information from each employee's server reconciliation should be transferred to the sales reconciliation, illustrated in Exhibit 9. The sales reconciliation is a summary of the server reconciliations and should be prepared by a manager or bookkeeper. This form is the basis for calculating the day's bank deposits. Consideration should be given to opening a bank account where only the PST and GST/HST collected are deposited. This will ensure the funds will be available for payment to the government.

The sales reconciliation form is completed as follows:

➤ Each server is listed in the 'Server' column.

➤ The amount of the server's deposit are copied from the server reconciliation and are reported by method of payment. The total deposit is written in the 'Total' column.

➤ The server's total sales, taken from the cash register tape, is reported in the 'Z Reading' column.

➤ The difference between the actual deposit and theoretical deposit ('Z' reading) is entered in the 'Variance' column.

➤ The amounts written in the 'Average Check' and 'Voids' columns are copied directly from the server's reconciliation.

➤ The sum of each column (except 'Average Check') is entered in the bottom row.

After every server reconciliation has been entered on the sales reconciliation, the total of the 'Cash' column is entered in the bottom left corner as the total 'Cash Deposit' for the day. Any other funds (e.g. cheque payment from credit card company) received during the day are listed below the cash deposit, and are included in the day's deposit.

The handling of credit card deposits varies by restaurant. Management should speak with the restaurant's credit card account managers to determine how the deposits should be made.

Tapes from the cash register and the server reconciliations should be attached to the sales reconciliation for tracking purposes.

Exhibit 9

59

Chapter Two

Sales Reconciliation Summary

DATE _____													
Server	# of guests served	MC	VISA	Amex	House Charge	Other	Total	'Z' Reading	Variance	Average Check	Voids
TOTAL											

Cash Deposits _____
Other Deposits _____
Total Deposits _____

Sales receipts ledger

The sales receipts ledger, illustrated in Exhibit 10, should be updated daily based on information in the sales reconciliation and attached register tapes. This ledger summarizes the restaurant's sales, receipts, and taxes collected for a period of up to 31 days. The sales receipts ledger is completed as follows:

➤ Write the date in the 'Date' column. This step is necessary for restaurants using a four-week cycle, where the first day of the period is not necessarily the first day of the month.

➤ In the 'Description' column write in the day of the week, or pertinent comment(s) (e.g. civic holiday).

➤ Total sales (including taxes) are transferred from the sales reconciliation and are reported by method of payment in the 'Total Revenue Including Tax' columns. The columns are then added together and the result is placed in the 'Total' column.

➤ Total sales (net of taxes) are reported by category of sale (food, beverage, sundry). This information should be available from the cash register's summary report.

➤ Taxes collected are broken down and reported in the 'PST-Food', 'PST-Liq' (Liquor), and 'GST/HST' columns. The total taxes collected during the day are reported in the 'Total' column.

The sales receipts ledger should be totaled at the end of every reporting period and the balances for each account should be posted to the general ledger.

Exhibit 10

61

Chapter Two

Sales Receipts Ledger

Date and Description	Total Revenue Including Taxes								Sales Breakdown				Taxes Collected		
	Cash	Visa	MC	Amex	House	Other	Total	Food	Bev	Sun	PSTF	PSTB	GST/HST	Total
1														
2														
3														
4														
5														
6														
7														
8														
9														
10														
11														
12														
13														
14														
15														
16														
17														
18														
19														
20														
21														
22														
23														
24														
25														
26														
27														
28														
29														
30														
31														
TOTAL														

Accounts receivable sub-ledger

A restaurant may wish to establish credit accounts for certain customers. It is important that a control system be in place whereby only management can authorize the opening of a credit account and credit limits be established for each account. A sub-ledger is opened for each customer with a credit account, illustrated in Exhibit 11, and should be filed in alphabetical order in a binder. Any sales that are not paid for in full (e.g. by cash, credit card, or cheque) at the time of the transaction are reported in the accounts receivable sub-ledger.

The customer's name, address and telephone number should be recorded at the top of the accounts receivable sub-ledger. A sequential account number should be assigned to each customer. A simple five column format can be used to record Purchases on Credit, Invoice Amount, Payments Received, and Balance. A bi-weekly, or monthly, invoice should be sent to all customers with outstanding balances. The amount of the invoice is recorded in the appropriate column. When the payment is received, the account is credited by that amount.

Management, or the bookkeeper, should review all the accounts receivable sub-ledgers on a monthly basis to ensure that accounts with invoices that are 30 days old are followed up. An example of how to follow up on receivables that are more than 30 days old is to mail (email) the customer a copy of the unpaid invoice along with a letter requesting payment. If the invoice remains unpaid 15 days after sending the reminder letter, management could phone the customer to request payment.

Exhibit 11

Accounts Receivable Sub-ledger

| Name: _____ Account #: _____ |
| Address: _____ Phone # _____ |

Date	Invoice #	Invoice Amt.	Payment	Balance

Cash float control

Cash register floats, petty cash floats and server change floats can be controlled by restricting access to the funds to specific individuals and by requiring receipts to support the use of these floats.

The purpose of a petty cash float and a system for controlling disbursements is discussed in the cash control section in Chapter Three.

If the restaurant issues a cash float to cashiers, bartenders, or servers, the cash register and server change floats should be accounted for as follows:

➤   When the float is first established, the cash disbursement is recorded in the cash disbursements ledger by crediting the bank account and debiting the petty cash account.

➤   When receipts are submitted for reimbursement of the fund, the cash disbursement is again recorded in the cash disbursements ledger as a credit to the bank account and a debit to the appropriate expense account.

Purchases, Payables and Payments

The purpose of the purchases, payables and payments system is to keep track of outstanding invoices, and to record those invoices which have been paid. Cash disbursements are made to purchase:

- ➤ food and beverage products;

- ➤ goods and services associated with operating the restaurant (e.g. rent, utilities); and,

- ➤ property, plant and equipment.

All of these purchases flow through the purchases, payables and payments system. Cash disbursements are also made for employee salaries and wages, but are accounted for in the payroll system.

Accounts payable sub-ledger

A simple method of keeping track of unpaid invoices is to file them by payment due date in an accordion file. If cheques are normally prepared weekly, the person in charge of making payments would go to the appropriate dates in the accordion file, remove the invoices, and write the cheques. The cheques are then recorded in the cash disbursements ledger. When an invoice is paid, the invoice should be marked paid, and the cheque number and date should be written on it. This avoids the possibility of double paying the same invoice.

When preparing the financial statements this sub-ledger is reviewed and all unpaid invoices relating to goods and services received in the reporting period are reported as 'accounts payable' in the general journal. After the financial statements are prepared, this entry should be reversed to ensure that invoices are not double counted when subsequently paid.

Cash disbursements ledger

When invoices are paid they should be recorded in the cash disbursements ledger, illustrated in Exhibit 12. A cash disbursements ledger should be set up for each of the restaurant's bank accounts.

Exhibit 12

65

Chapter Two

Cash Disbursement Ledger

Bank																	
Account			#														
Date	Payee	Inv #	Cheque #	Amt	GST/HST paid	Cost of Sales Food	Bev	Occupancy Exp	Operate Exp	Gen & Admin	Royalty Fee	Adv	Entertainment	Interest	Other Amount	Acc't

This ledger should be organized chronologically and by cheque number, thereby maintaining control over cheques (which should be sequentially numbered). The ledger is completed as follows:

- ➤ The date of the cheque is recorded in the first column.

- ➤ The supplier's name and invoice number are recorded in the 'Payee' and 'Invoice #' columns, respectively.

- ➤ The cheque number and amount are recorded in the 'Cheque #' and 'Cheque Amount' columns, respectively.

- ➤ The amount of GST/HST paid is recorded separately. This will assist in calculating the amount of GST/HST owed to the government. The amount of GST/HST owed is the 'GST/HST collected from customers' less the 'GST/HST paid to suppliers'.

- ➤ The net expense (not including GST/HST) is reported in the 'Expense' columns in the cash disbursements ledger. These columns correspond to the expenses in the income statement:

  - – Cost of sales - food
  - – Cost of sales - beverages
  - – Cost of sales - sundry
  - – Occupancy
  - – Operating
  - – General and administrative
  - – Marketing
  - – Entertainment
  - – Royalty fee
  - – Interest
  - – Other

➤ The 'Other' columns are used for recording the account number, and the amount of the cheque, (net of GST/HST) of expenditures made for expenses not reported in the income statement. The GST/HST paid is reported in the 'GST/HST' column. For instance, a purchase of a new table for the restaurant would be recorded in this column as an addition to 'Furniture, fixtures and equipment' (account number 1504).

The system allows for a simple breakdown of costs into these basic categories. This information should be sufficient for smaller sized restaurants. For medium sized or larger restaurants further breakdowns may be required and can be achieved through the use of sub-ledgers. Each of the expense categories in the cash disbursements ledger can have a sub-ledger breaking out costs into detailed accounts. For example a sub-ledger for 'Cost of sales - food' would break down this general category into the detail outlined in the chart of accounts (purchases of produce, dairy, meats, poultry, seafood, bread and dried and canned goods).

The cash disbursements ledger should be totaled at the end of every reporting period, and the balances in each account should be transferred to the general ledger.

Payroll

I n the payroll system it will be necessary to maintain a record of employment of all employees hired by the restaurant. It will also be necessary to maintain a record of all salaries, wages and benefits paid to employees. This information is recorded in the payroll register.

The payroll register may be organized by pay period, or by employee. If separate records are maintained for each employee, it is easier to process the cumulative pay and deduction information for T4 preparation at the end of the calendar year.

Payroll register – salaried employees

The payroll register - salaried employees, illustrated in Exhibit 13, is completed as follows:

- ➤ The register assumes that employees will be paid bi-weekly and, thus, the first column lists the 26 periods.

- ➤ The date and amount of the cheque are listed in the 'Date' and 'Cheque #' columns respectively.

- ➤ The employee's total salary for the pay period is entered in the 'Gross Salaries' column.

- ➤ The total 'Taxable Benefits' (e.g. staff meals, automobiles) are entered in the next column.

- ➤ The employee deductions for the period are recorded in the 'CPP' (Canada Pension Plan), 'EI' (Employment Insurance), and 'Tax' (Income Tax) columns.

- ➤ The difference between the gross salary and the deductions is the salary earned in the pay period and is recorded in the 'Net Pay' column.

Exhibit 13

69

Chapter Two

Payroll Register—Salaried Employee

Employee Name																			
Pay period	Date	Cheq #	Gross Salary	Taxable Benefits	Employee Deductions			Net Pay	Employer Remittances				Other		Total to Remit	Vacation Pay
					CPP	EI	Tax		CPP	EI	WC	EHT	Acct #	Amt		
1																
2																
3																
4																
5																
6																
7																
8																
9																
10																
11																
12																
13																
14																
15																
16																
17																
18																
19																
20																
21																
22																
23																
24																
25																
26																
Total																

Employer's remittances for the pay period are recorded in the 'CPP' (Canada Pension Plan), 'EI' (Employment Insurance), 'WC' (Workers' Compensation), 'EHT' (Employer Health Tax) columns.

➤ Other earnings (e.g. bonuses) or deductions (e.g. repayment of loan) are recorded in the 'Other' columns.

➤ The sum of the 'Net Pay' and 'Other - Amount' columns is equal to the amount of the pay cheque and is recorded in the 'Total to Remit' column.

➤ The employee's accrued vacation pay for the period is calculated (e.g. four percent of gross salary) and recorded in the 'Vacation Pay' column.

Payroll register – hourly employees

The payroll register - hourly employees, illustrated in Exhibit 14, is similar to that of salaried employees except for the calculation of gross wages. Columns for hours worked, hourly rates, and overtime are necessary in the hourly employees' register in order to compute their wages for the pay period. This information should be obtained from time cards, or sign-in/sign-out sheets. Once the amount of the gross wage earned has been calculated, the payroll register for hourly employees is completed in the same manner as for salaried employees.

Exhibit 14

71

Payroll Register—Hourly Employees

Employee Name																				
Pay period	Date	Cheque #	Wage Rate Reg.	Wage Rate O/T	Hours Worked Reg	Hours Worked O/T	Gross Wages	Taxable Benefits	Employee Deductions CPP	Employee Deductions EI	Employee Deductions Tax	Net Pay	Employer Remittances CPP	Employer Remittances EI	Employer Remittances WC	Employer Remittances EHT	Other Acct #	Other Amt	Total to Remit	Vacation Pay
1																				
2																				
3																				
4																				
5																				
6																				
7																				
8																				
9																				
10																				
11																				
12																				
13																				
14																				
15																				
16																				
17																				
18																				
19																				
20																				
21																				
22																				
23																				
24																				
25																				
26																				
Total																				

Payroll register - summary

The two payroll registers, described previously, are set up by employee, and summarize an employee's full salaries, wages and benefits for one year. While this method simplifies the preparation of employees' T4s at the end of the year, it does not allow for the easy calculation of total salaries, wages, and benefits for a period. The payroll register - summary, illustrated in Exhibit 15, is used to calculate the period's salaries, wages and benefits expenses.

The payroll register - summary should not require a great deal of time to complete, and should be filled in as follows:

> ➤ List all the employees' names in the 'Employee Name' column.

> ➤ Transfer the gross wages/salaries, employee deductions, employer remittances, other, and vacation pay to the appropriate columns.

> ➤ Total each column.

The total salaries, wages and benefits for the reporting period is the sum of the total of these columns:

> ➤ 'Gross Salaries' + 'Employer Remittances' (CPP, EI, WC, EHT) + 'Other Amt' + 'Vacation Pay'

The total employer's remittances is the amount which must be remitted along with the employees' withholdings for the period. The portion of the total salaries, wages and benefits (calculated above) that is not paid out to employees is reported as a payroll liability on the balance sheet. The chart of accounts (Appendix) details the various types of payroll liabilities (e.g. Employment Insurance, Canada Pension Plan).

Exhibit 15

73

Chapter Two

Payroll Register—Summary

Pay Period _____

Employee Name	Gross Salary	Taxable Benefits	Employee Deductions			Net Pay	Employer Remittances				Other Amount	Vacation Pay
			CPP	EI	Tax		CPP	EI	WC	EHT		

Inventory

Purchases of inventory items, including food and beverage, are recorded in the cash disbursements ledger, as part of the purchases, payable and payments system. However, in order to determine the cost of the food and beverage sold in the period it is also necessary to know the beginning and ending inventory for the period. This information is provided by the inventory system.

A restaurant may employ one of two systems to keep track of its inventory: a periodic inventory system, or a perpetual inventory system.

Periodic inventory system

In a periodic inventory system there is no running balance of the inventory on-hand. At the end of the reporting period, inventory is counted and the cost of sales is calculated as follows:

cost of sales = beginning inventory + purchases – ending inventory

The weakness of the periodic inventory system is the lack of control over items being removed from inventory. Since the accounting records do not tell management what should be in inventory, there is no way to know whether theft or excessive spoilage of inventory is occurring.

Accounting entries under a periodic inventory system are made at the end of a reporting period in the general journal. An example of these entries is shown in the sample general journal (see Exhibit 16).

Perpetual inventory system

A perpetual inventory system requires that all movements in and out of inventory be recorded in the accounting records so that a running balance of the inventory is maintained. Thus, closing entries at the end of a reporting period (required under the periodic inventory system) are not needed.

Beverage inventories should be maintained on a perpetual inventory system because of the high unit cost. Chapter Three has a detailed explanation of the 'bin card system' which is a simple method of maintaining perpetual inventory records for beverages.

Regular inventory counts are still required under a perpetual inventory system to ensure that the system is operating correctly. Any variances between inventory counts and the perpetual inventory system should be followed up by management to determine the cause of the discrepancy.

General Journal

The purpose of the general journal, illustrated in Exhibit 16, is to record non-cash transactions and adjustments needed to prepare financial statements. These adjustments are required so that the income statement and balance sheet conform to the principle of matching revenues with expenses. The entries commonly made in the general journal are discussed below:

Food inventory adjustments

When food inventories are maintained on a periodic inventory system, certain entries are required to be made in the general journal at the end of the reporting period. The sample general journal shows an example of entries made to:

➤ clear out the purchases accounts to the cost of food sold account;

➤ back out the entry setting up the previous period's inventory; and,

➤ set up the entry for this period's inventory on hand.

Depreciation adjustments

As noted in the balance sheet discussion of property, plant and equipment, it is necessary to make an entry in the general journal to record the amount of depreciation during the reporting period for each class of property, plant and equipment. An example of this type of entry is shown in the sample general journal. Depreciation expense is recorded, and added to the balance of accumulated depreciation. The asset's original cost and accumulated depreciation are reported on the balance sheet.

Accruals

At the end of the reporting period it is necessary to go through the accounts payable ledger and report the unpaid invoices as expenses and accounts payable. The sample general journal shows the reversal of the entry setting up payables for the previous reporting period, and a new entry is made for the current period.

It will also be necessary to accrue those expenses for which there are no invoices, such as payroll expenses (if the payroll date does not coincide with the reporting date), interest expenses, and income taxes. Again, expenses accrued in the prior period should be reversed.

It is also necessary to record accounts receivables, based on amounts outstanding in the accounts receivable sub-ledger. These outstanding amounts should be recorded as revenue in the income statement, and set up as accounts receivable in the balance sheet. As with accounts payable, the entry setting up receivables for the previous reporting period is reversed and a new entry is made for the current period.

Exhibit 16
General Journal

Entry	Description		Account #	Amount	
Date				Debit	Credit
Entry #1	Purchases - Food		5000	421,764	
Dec, 31, 20x2	Purchases	Produce	5001		69,135
		dairy	5002		58,026
		meats	5003		80,903
		poultry	5004		70,940
		seafood	5005		61,330
		bread	5006		28,310
		dried & canned	5007		49,590
		misc.	5008		3,530
	To close out purchases account under periodic inventory system.				
	Purchases - Food		5000	10,579	
	Inventory Food		1200		10,579
	To reverse entry setting up food inventory at end of last year under periodic inventory system.				
	Inventory - Food		1200	9,843	
	Cost of Goods Sold - Food		5000		9,843
	To record inventory balance at end of year based on physical count.				
Entry # 2					
Dec, 31, 20x2	Depreciation - Leasehold Improvement		5853	15,645	
	Accumulated Depreciation - Leasehold Improvement		1533		15,645
	To record depreciation expense on leasehold improvements for the year.				
Entry # 3					
Dec, 31, 20x2	Marketing expenses		5600	6,479	
	Operating expenses		5400	16,773	
	General & Administrative		5500	3,888	
	Accounts payable		2000		27,140
	To set up accounts payable per accounts payable ledger.				
Entry # 4					
Dec, 31, 20x2	Accounts Payable		2000	29,480	
	Marketing expenses		5600		7,890
	Operating expenses		5400		18,451
	General & Administrative		5500		3,139
	To reverse prior period entry setting up accounts payable.				
Entry # 5					
Dec, 31, 20x2	Interest - bank loan		5803	2,580	
	Accrued expenses		2300		2,580
	To accrue interest expense to the end of the year.				
	Doubtful Accounts expense- General & Admin		5513	800	
	Allowance for doubtful accounts		1103		800
	To set up the allowance for doubtful accounts or the period.				

It will also be necessary to record an allowance for doubtful accounts in the general journal. At the end of each reporting period it is necessary to review all accounts receivable and estimate an amount to be set aside as a provision for receivables that will likely not be collected. This amount is referred to as the allowance for doubtful accounts. The amount should be based upon the historical experience of the restaurant. In a new operation, industry statistics from fellow restaurant operators or your restaurant association may be used until the restaurant has established its own collection history. The expense is recorded in the income statement under general and administration. Accounts receivables are presented in the balance sheet net of the allowance for doubtful accounts.

When specific accounts are found to be 'not collectible' they should be written off (sales should be reduced by this amount and the receivable should be reversed from the books of account.) In the event the amount is collected in a future period the amount should be recorded as sales revenue in the period it is received.

Prepaid expenses

Any amounts paid for services or goods to be received in future periods should be set up as a prepaid expense on the balance sheet. The example used in the discussion of prepaid expenses in the balance sheet was insurance expense, where the premium has been paid, but the period of coverage has not expired as of the reporting date.

Prepaid expenses set up in the previous reporting period should be reversed before making the entry to record the current period prepaid.

Year-end closing entries

At the end of the year, certain entries are required to 'close out' the income statement accounts which are meant to accumulate information on an annual basis. The income statement accounts are closed out to retained earnings, and thus the retained earnings account is increased (decreased) by the amount of net income (net loss) for the year.

After the closing entries are made the income statement accounts should have a zero balance, ready to accumulate transactions for the upcoming year.

General Ledger

The general ledger is a complete listing of the accounts identified in the chart of accounts, and is normally organized in a binder format. The accounts are organized by the account numbers detailed in the chart of accounts (Appendix). At the end of every reporting period the balances from the:

> ➤ sales receipts ledger;

> ➤ cash disbursements ledger;

> ➤ payroll registers; and,

> ➤ general journal

are added to the appropriate accounts in the general ledger. The new total for each account forms the basis for that reporting period's financial statements.

Trial Balance

At the end of a reporting period a trial balance, illustrated in Exhibit 17, of the general ledger is prepared. The trial balance lists all the ledger accounts and their net credit or net debit balance. These balances should be adjusted to reflect any end-of-period adjusting entries. If a restaurant has a significant number of adjusting entries at the end of a reporting period, it may be helpful to add an 'Adjusted Trial Balance' column (to report the balances from the general ledger) and an 'Adjusting Entry' column (to report the adjusting entries). The sum of these two columns is reported in the 'Trial Balance' columns (i.e. debits, credits). Once the trial balance is completed, the total debits should equal total credits.

Note that the trial balance reports the retained earnings at the beginning of the period. In addition, income tax expense can only be recorded after the income statement has been completed.

Exhibit 17

81

Chapter Two

Trial Balance

Item	Debit	Credit
Balance Sheet		
Cash	123,820	
Accounts Receivable	6,927	
Inventory – Food	9,843	
Inventory – Beverage	10,269	
Inventory – Other	7,322	
Prepaid Expense	5,444	
Deposit	4,600	
Land	100,000	
Building	145,794	
Accumulated Depreciation	27,044	118,750
Furniture, Fixture and Equipment	445,084	
Accumulated Depreciation	243,060	202,024
Leasehold Equipment	156,450	
Accumulated Depreciation	62,580	93,870
Automobiles	88,921	
Accumulated Depreciation	67,571	21,350
Accounts Payable		27,140
Deposits		10,500
Sales Tax & GST/HST		13,296
Accrued Expenses		5,492
Accrued Interest Liability		2,000
Payroll Liability		4,900
Bank Loan		135,275
Due to Shareholders		10,000
Common Shares		240,000
Preferred Shares		113,000
Retained Earnings		114,399
Dividends	60,000	
Income Statement		
Sales Food		1,240,482
Sales Beverage		304,482
Sales Sundry		66,052
Cost of Sales – Food	421,764	
Cost of Sales – Beverage	109,005	
Cost of Sales – Sundry	29,856	
Salaries, Wages & Benefits	512,303	
Occupancy Expense	134,871	
Operating Expenses	83,945	
General and Admin Expense	49,941	
Marketing Expense	45,108	
Entertainment Expense	14,499	
Interest Expense	10,550	
Depreciation Expense	81,551	
Income Tax Expense *	29,406	
Balance	2,287,018	2,287,018

* Recorded after the Income Statement has been prepared

Chapter Three

Internal Controls

The first two chapters of this book have outlined a standard format and methodology by which management can develop financial statements. This standardization will provide a clear and easy-to-use format and will allow for statistical comparison between restaurants and to industry averages (contained in the CRFA's Foodservice Operations Report, for example).

This chapter outlines a variety of methodologies which, if implemented in a restaurant, should assist in the reduction of major cost areas and, thus, increase net income. The focus is on the control of prime costs (food, beverage and labour), as experience indicates that a significant number of failures in the restaurant and foodservice industry are due to the lack of proper internal control systems for these areas. Additionally, the last section of this chapter deals with some basic cash control procedures.

Prime costs are defined as all the direct costs associated with serving food and beverage and with labour in a restaurant or foodservice environment. As indicated in Chapter One, prime costs account for the largest portion of any restaurant's operating expense. Costs vary by restaurant type, but generally food costs range from 25 percent to 40 percent of food sales, beverage costs range from 24 percent to 35 percent of beverage sales, and labour costs range from 22 percent to 30 percent of total sales.

A restaurateur should target a 60 percent to 65 percent gross margin on total sales after accounting for food and beverage costs, and a minimum of 30 percent gross margin after labour cost is accounted for. If these operating ratios are met, it is possible for a restaurant to achieve an operating income of 10 percent or more.

A restaurant must have a minimum level of sales to survive. If restaurant sales cannot support the operational costs, then a conceptual review or a market assessment should be undertaken. However, if a restaurant's sales approach or exceed the industry average, and if the operation maintains strong prime cost controls, an annual profit should be achievable.

This section is divided into the following four sub-sections:

- ➤ Food Cost Controls;

- ➤ Beverage Cost Controls;

- ➤ Labour Cost Controls; and,

- ➤ Cash Controls.

Each sub-section details the pertinent control systems for each area. Where the controls are the same for both food and beverage, we have documented the control system in the Food Cost Controls section and written '(Beverage)' in the system's title.

Computerization

This chapter describes manual internal control systems which can be used by restaurants or foodservice operations. The principles underlying these manual systems are the same as those used in computerized systems. The data collected and the type of information generated are virtually the same in the two types of systems. Accordingly, as with the previous two chapters on accounting, the majority of the manual systems described in this chapter can be computerized.

There are a variety of reasons why this chapter discusses manual internal control systems, including:

- ➤ The internal control systems used by many independent restaurateurs will likely be a hybrid of manual and computerized systems. The reason for this hybrid is that manual systems are easy and inexpensive to implement and computerized systems, once implemented, are generally less time consuming to manage and may provide more timely information.

- ➤ A detailed discussion on manual internal control systems will provide the reader with a thorough understanding of how the systems work and what they are intended to accomplish. This understanding will help the reader determine which internal control systems should be computerized, and if the system is to be computerized, what the software's capabilities should be.

➤ Discussing current software programs is frequently not relevant due to the rapidity with which technology changes and, therefore, programs become outdated or discontinued. We believe that the principles underlying the manual systems will continue to be relevant and that changes in technology will primarily impact the processing and/or manipulation of the data.

There are numerous electronic and computerized systems that can be used to control almost every aspect of a restaurant operation. Prior to purchasing any computerized or electronic system, management should clearly define their expectations of the internal control system.

Management should speak to fellow restaurant operators and get their opinion as to available computer equipment and establish what they use and what is useful. In addition, management should meet with several POS representatives, talk to local computer dealers, and call industry associations such as the Canadian Restaurant and Foodservices Association for their recommendations. They should then select the system which provides them with the desired cost control benefits.

Management should also do a cost analysis of the proposed investment in order to ensure that the projected savings provide a satisfactory payback on the capital investment and labour costs of implementing and managing the system.

Food Cost Controls

Food cost, generally the largest expense in the restaurant and foodservice industry, is defined as all product costs associated with the production of meals. Food cost includes the cost of ingredients, shipping and handling, special packaging, pick up, delivery and rush charges, and is reduced by discounts available from early payment, manufacturer's rebate and/or volume purchases.

Food costs can be controlled and maintained through the use of various techniques which can assist management in the reduction of waste and theft, while allowing for improvements in purchasing, receiving and production. This section concentrates on the benefits provided through the implementation of:

- ➤ standard recipes;
- ➤ product specifications;
- ➤ supplier comparisons;
- ➤ purchase and receiving procedures;
- ➤ storage methodologies;
- ➤ inventory control;
- ➤ sales mix analysis;
- ➤ forecasting;
- ➤ theoretical food cost;
- ➤ variance reports;
- ➤ kitchen waste reports; and,
- ➤ guest check controls.

In addition, this section will present various forms and reports that are integral in the implementation of these food cost controls. The matrix, following, details the various forms and reports used, identifies who is responsible for completing the form/reports, and specifies the frequency with which they are completed.

REPORT NAME	FILLED OUT BY	HOW OFTEN
Standard recipes	kitchen manager	once per recipe
Product specifications	kitchen manager	once per item
Supplier comparison	manager	every three months
Purchase & receiving	purchaser & receiver	every order
Short form inventory	kitchen & general manager	once per cycle
Long form inventory	kitchen & general manager	once per cycle
Purchase log book	kitchen manager	daily
Sales mix analysis	manager	daily & weekly
Theoretical food cost	kitchen & general manager	once per cycle
Variance report	kitchen manager	daily
Kitchen waste	kitchen staff	daily
Guest check control	manager	daily

Computerized food control systems

The most common computerized food control systems are point-of-sales systems (POS), or electronic cash registers (ECR). These systems range in price from under $1,000 for a basic system to tens of thousands of dollars for the most sophisticated and fully integrated systems. The vast majority of restaurants are computerized with, at a minimum, a basic system which consists of an electronic cash register located in the front-of-the-house. The ECR is a stand-alone computer system which can track all sales transactions, and break down sales into food, liquor, and applicable taxes.

The POS systems in the market vary in sophistication and can be customized to various degrees to meet the needs of the operation and management. The most sophisticated systems have multiple-use input units located throughout the restaurant at fixed points or use multiple server hand-held units. The input stations are connected via remote printers to the kitchen and bar areas; all the data collected is stored on a central processing unit, generally located in the management office. These sophisticated POS systems will perform all the tasks of the basic system described above and a plethora of other tasks. For example, the POS may detail the number of customers each server served, the server's and restaurant's average check, and may provide a detailed sales mix report (i.e. unit sales by item). These systems may also allow the manager to input standard recipes, purchases and inventory counts in order to generate updated menu and inventory costs on a periodic basis.

Sophisticated POS systems can be programmed to automatically project dollar and unit sales for each menu item. Based on these projections, the system can then generate the purchase orders necessary to prepare those meals. The technology exists for the POS to process the order and transmit it to the supplier.

In addition, many of these systems have built in time clocks where employees sign-in and sign-out. At the end of the period the total hours worked, the gross wages, deductions, and net pay are calculated. This information is then printed on a labour report and the more sophisticated systems can print the employees' pay cheques.

Sophisticated POS systems can generate end-of-period reports of up to 50 pages. Once a restaurant's management has determined their POS needs, they should meet with representatives of several POS companies and select a system which matches their needs.

In addition to the POS systems outlined above, there are numerous internal control systems designed for restaurants. These systems address various areas, including: labour control, cash control, food cost control, inventory control, beverage control, and accounting.

For example, there are food cost control software programs which can be used in conjunction with an inexpensive ECR or POS to provide sophisticated controls and possible cost savings.

One Canadian program, for example, provides full menu explosion, inventory control and waste management procedures. The program enables management to input their full raw ingredient list, and through a 'point and shoot' process, develop standard recipes costed out to the penny. The program will automatically update the recipe costs every time the cost of a raw ingredient is changed, thus saving considerable time. The program also converts metric to imperial measurement and weight to measure automatically, eliminating work which is painstaking and time consuming when calculated manually.

The program goes on to provide closing inventory data collection forms and will generate inventory reports which yield information on the use and cost of each raw ingredient on an ingredient by ingredient basis. Additional information on the inventory report includes: cost and value of goods sold, cost and value of goods on hand, actual food cost, food cost percentage and product turnover information.

By inputting into the program the data from the POS sales mix reports, management can obtain a theoretical food cost report (the benchmark to compare the actual food cost) and the performance assurance rating (PAR). PAR is a sophisticated menu analysis technique which evaluates each menu item's contribution to the operation's overall profit. Finally, the program creates detailed waste reports enabling management to pinpoint specific areas of concern.

This type of program is available from several suppliers in Canada and the United States. Over time operators who implement manual systems and realize the benefits should consider automation to reduce the time involved maintaining a manual system.

Standard recipes

An important aspect of food cost control is the development and use of standard recipes. Standard recipes allow for portion control of products, assist in providing consistency in the preparation of food, allow for the calculation of food cost and food cost percentage for each item and are, in essence, the heart of a successful food cost control program.

Standard recipes should be developed for every item a restaurant serves. There are two types of standard recipes: sub-recipes and recipes. The difference between the two is:

> ➤ Sub-recipes are for items which are made by a restaurant but not sold as a menu item (e.g. a batch recipe).

> ➤ Recipes are for items which are made by the restaurant and sold as a menu item. A recipe can consist of raw ingredients and sub-recipes, while sub-recipes are usually made from raw ingredients only.

For example, a restaurant may make a gallon of soup, but sells an eight-ounce bowl of soup which is accompanied by a few crackers. The batch of soup would be the sub-recipe while the bowl of soup and crackers would be the recipe. If a restaurant were to sell hamburgers, the sub-recipe would be a 20-pound batch of ground beef mixed with eggs and onions which yields 40, eight-ounce hamburger patties. (NOTE: In 2009 in Canada, customers still view product in imperial measures while vendors sell in both imperial and metric. Each restaurant should use what the chef, management and customers are most comfortable with). The recipe for a hamburger would consist of one hamburger patty from the sub-recipe plus a bun, French fries, one or two ounces of condiments and a garnish.

In order to prepare a standard recipe, management should follow these steps and use the report illustrated in Exhibit 18.

> ➤ Write the name of the recipe, or sub-recipe, in the 'Item' line.

> ➤ Enter the date of the update (e.g. date when ingredient costs were last revised) in the 'Date' line.

> ➤ If it is a recipe, write in the item's selling price on the appropriate line.

> ➤ Write the number of portions in the recipe/sub-recipe in the 'Yield' line.

> ➤ List under the 'Raw Ingredient' column all the raw ingredients (or sub-recipes) including all spices, sauces, oils for cooking, and condiments that may be used at time of service.

> ➤ In the 'Weight/Measure' column list the quantity (measure, volume or weight) of each item which is to be used. For example, eight ounces, two teaspoons, five fluid ounces, etc.

Exhibit 18
Standard Recipe Cost Report

| Item: _____ | | Date: _____ | |
| Selling Price: _____ | | Yield: _____ | |

Raw Ingredient	Weight/Measure	Cost Per Unit	Extended Cost
		Total Cost	
		Portion Cost	
		Food Cost %	

Preparation Instructions:

_____
_____
_____
_____
_____
_____
_____
_____

Garnish

_____
_____

- ➤ In the 'Cost per Unit' column list the cost per purchase unit (e.g. $5.00 per pound). The unit of measure (e.g. ounces) in the 'Cost per Unit' and 'Weight/Measure' columns should be the same.

- ➤ The 'Extended Cost' column is used to calculate the cost of each ingredient in the recipe. In order to do this, divide the quantity used by the number of units per purchase unit and multiply this number by the cost per unit.

- ➤ Calculate the sum of the 'Extended Cost' column and write this amount in the 'Total Cost' box.

- ➤ Divide the 'Total Cost' amount by the 'Yield' (number of portions) of the recipe and enter this amount in the 'Portion Cost' box.

- ➤ Divide the 'Portion Cost' amount by the item's selling price (for recipes only) to determine the recipe's theoretical 'Food Cost %'.

- ➤ At the bottom of the page, write out the preparation instructions in the clearest and most simple manner possible. The instructions should be written in bullet form, with each bullet describing a specific step in the preparation.

Once the standard recipes are developed, a complete set should be kept in the office, while a set without prices could be kept in the kitchen for use by staff. This should ensure consistency in preparation and portion size from day to day and cook to cook. Additionally, standard recipes provide a side benefit to labour control as they will reduce staff training time. New staff should become rapidly familiar with the preparation of the various food products by following standard recipes.

Standard portioning will take effect with standard recipes, as each recipe will provide the portion which should be used. Ultimately, however, it is the cook's responsibility to ensure that the exact portions are used. Further, standard recipes allow for effective costing practices. Every three months, at a minimum, all the ingredients' costs should be updated, and the recipes should be re-costed to ensure that the restaurant is still maintaining its desired food cost percentage.

To make life a little easier, there are several computer software packages available which can help implement and track these calculations. This will make periodic updates of costs extremely fast and easy.

Purchasing

Another very important aspect in maintaining the desired food cost is the control and use of purchasing, receiving and storage techniques. Each of these areas will be addressed separately, although the control report used for purchasing and receiving is the same.

When purchasing items for a restaurant, management must take into consideration the restaurant's needs, a product's shelf life, current inventory, minimum purchase requirements, delivery schedules, volume discounts and storage space available.

The first step in effective purchasing is to select the 'right' suppliers. Management should follow the process detailed below in selecting suppliers:

- ➤ Develop a set of product specifications for every raw ingredient used in the restaurant.

- ➤ Circulate these product specifications to various suppliers in order to obtain their quotes.

- ➤ Assess the bids on various criteria (e.g. price, delivery).

- ➤ Select suppliers for each group of products.

Product specification

The product specification sheet, illustrated in Exhibit 19, should detail the exact quality and size of all products needed by the restaurant.

The product specification sheet is extremely important for any foodservice operation as it clearly defines the raw ingredients which will be used. Product specifications include a description of the product, the grade, size, weight or size of container and quality of product to be used. The specification is then sent out to suppliers so that they know on what to bid, what to send and what will be accepted by the restaurant.

In order to accurately complete the product specification sheet management should:

➤ Enter the name of the raw ingredient next to the heading 'Product'.

➤ On the 'Date' line enter the date when the product specification was developed or revised.

➤ On the second line enter the standard 'Purchase Unit'. This usually indicates the quantity or measure in which the restaurant purchases (e.g. pound, kilogram, gallon, litre).

➤ On the 'Type of Container' line enter the type of packaging for the product (e.g. box, bag, pail).

➤ On the 'Weight or Size' line enter the standard purchase quantity (e.g. 50 pounds, four litres).

➤ Under 'Product Description' write a description of the product which the restaurant will use. The product description should be based on the descriptions in guides provided by Agriculture and Agri-food Canada, product marketing boards, and suppliers.

For example, a product description for eggs could read:

– Grade A, clean unbroken shell;

– white should be clear and firm; and,

– yolk outline slightly defined and practically free from defects.

A product description for salmon may read as:

– fresh, not frozen, silver (coho) salmon;

– flesh colour of red to orange-red or light pink; and,

– moderately firm flesh texture.

Exhibit 19
Product Specification

Product	_____	Date	_____
Unit Size	_____	Type of Container	_____
Quote Required by	_____	Weight or Size	_____

Product Description

_____

_____

_____

_____

_____

_____

_____

_____

_____

Specification Approved by

Chef	_____	Date	_____
Manager	_____	Date	_____

Specifications Sent To

	Supplier	Contact	Phone
#1			
#2			
#3			

➤ The product specification sheet should be approved by both the chef and the manager.

➤ A copy of the top portion of the sheet is sent to suppliers. The date by which the quote should be returned should be indicated.

➤ A copy of the entire product specification sheet is kept by management. Notes should be made with regards to the suppliers contacted.

Through the creation of product specifications, a restaurant should save money. The restaurant will order beef with a certain fat content so that it receives the flavour required without the excess trim. The type of mushrooms used for soup may not have to be the same quality, or high cost, as mushrooms for a steak garnish. The specifications ensure that everyone involved in purchasing, supplying and receiving an order knows exactly what product is going to be used and what is acceptable.

Once the specifications are sent out, the quotes received should be placed on a supplier comparison report.

Supplier comparison report

Another effective methodology for controlling food costs is to maintain a supplier comparison report. While it is too time consuming to conduct a price comparison for every purchase order, it is cost effective to conduct a complete comparison every three months. Suppliers will frequently provide excellent prices to a new buyer in order to enhance their profile and obtain a new account. However, over time their prices may increase and may no longer be as attractive. By conducting a supplier comparison analysis every three months, management will receive new price schedules from all suppliers and will be able to determine the need for a change in suppliers or whether a new price should be negotiated.

When conducting a supplier comparison, inform each supplier that they are to provide a fixed price for, ideally, a 90-day period. Ensure that they have all the pertinent product specifications (and that they are providing a price based on the specifications). This will allow management to compare price quotes for similar products (apples to apples).

The supplier comparison report, illustrated in Exhibit 20, is quite easy to use.

➤ Enter the 'Category' of products being compared (meat, fish, dairy) on the first line of the report.

➤ Enter on the 'Date Completed' line the date the analysis was completed.

➤ The person conducting the analysis must sign the 'Analysis Conducted by' line. This indicates the person's involvement and responsibility for the accuracy of the document.

➤ In the 'Product' column enter all of the raw ingredients the restaurant uses in that category. For example, in the meat category enter all the meat items: ground beef lean, ground beef medium, New York steak 10 ounce, New York steak eight ounce, top sirloin butt, rack of lamb, etc.

➤ At the top of the next three columns write in the name of the suppliers and their phone numbers.

➤ Once the price lists are received, enter the supplier's price for each product and staple the supplier's price list to the back for quick reference.

Based upon the supplier comparison report, management must decide whether to switch suppliers or negotiate with the present supplier until a mutually satisfactory price can be obtained. Once management and the supplier have agreed to a price, circle it for quick reference. This will immediately indicate to the purchaser which supplier is to be used.

Exhibit 20
Supplier Comparison Report

Category _____

Date Completed _____

Analysis conducted _____

	Supplier #1	Supplier #2	Supplier #3
	Phone #	Phone #	Phone #
Product			

In order to purchase and receive effectively, the purchaser should use a purchase and receiving report, illustrated in Exhibit 21. One such report should be set up for each category of supplies (e.g. meats, groceries, fish, dairy, bakery). The purchase and receiving report then becomes the entire control sheet for the order.

The purchaser completes the first part of the purchase and receiving report in the following manner:

➤ The purchaser's name should be entered on the 'Ordered by' line at the top of the page and the date which the order was placed entered on the 'Date' line.

➤ Each product which is to be ordered should be listed in the 'Ingredient' column.

➤ To order effectively, the purchaser should know approximately how many units are on hand and estimate how many units will be needed prior to placing an order. Therefore, a cursory inventory should be taken prior to each order being placed. In order to do this enter the number of units on hand in the upper left hand corner of the 'Inventory' column.

➤ Estimate the number of units which the restaurant needs (read section on forecasting) and write this estimate in the right hand box under 'par'.

➤ Subtract the left hand number under 'Inventory' from the right hand number (forecasted needs) and write the result under the column headed 'Ordered'. The amount in the 'Ordered' column represents the additional stock the restaurant needs.

➤ As the purchaser orders ingredients from the supplier a tick should be placed in the 'X' column to indicate that the order was actually placed.

The purchase and receiving report is then sent to the receiver and is used as the control sheet for receiving the goods.

Exhibit 21
Purchasing and Receiving Report

Ordered by						
Received by						

Ingredient	Inventory		Ordered	x	Received	Missing	Rec/Del by
	On Hand	Par					

Ordered by _____ Date _____

Received by _____ Date _____

Receiving

Receiving is an extremely important part of any restaurant operation. It is likely that proper receiving procedures can reduce costs by one or two percent and this savings will drop directly to the bottom line. A restaurant which has $1 million in sales may be able to realize an additional $10,000 income annually by implementing proper receiving techniques.

To be effective, it is important to ensure that the receiving is handled by someone other than the purchaser, no matter how small the operation. The separation of these two tasks increases the control over what is being received and reduces the chance of theft.

The receiver should be someone who is knowledgeable about the quality of the food which goes out of the kitchen. This person should have a level of expertise with regards to food quality and production and, thus, be able to check the quality of the food received. Additionally, the receiver should have the authority to refuse food that is of inferior quality or which does not match the product specifications.

When the order arrives at the restaurant, the receiver will use the purchase and receiving report as the control sheet. The receiver should match the actual product received with the supplier invoice and the purchase and receiving report ensuring that:

> everything that was ordered was received;

> nothing was supplied which was not ordered;

> the quality and size of the products is what was ordered; and,

> only the products received are shown on the supplier's invoice.

The receiver should always check the order while the driver waits. Any changes to the invoice (e.g. the return of an inferior product) should be initialed by the driver who is acting as the supplier's agent.

It is good practice to have a receiving stamp that can be applied to the invoice/packing slip for the receiver to confirm and initial that the order was checked for quality, quantity, temperature and, as ordered.

Purchase and receiving report - receiving

The receiving portion of the purchase and receiving report is filled in as follows:

> In the column marked 'Received' the receiver should indicate that the items ordered in fact arrived at the restaurant. If the order is in good condition and meets with the product specifications, then a tick should be placed in the 'Received' column. If the receiver has any problems with the order, the problems should be marked in the 'Received' column.

➤ Under the 'Missing' column, the receiver enters the quantity that was short shipped, sent back or otherwise defective. It is very important that these items are clearly marked so that the purchaser will look for another source of product to make up for the missing items. Additionally, the short shipment should be clearly marked for the bookkeeper so that the invoice will be adjusted and payment will be made accordingly.

➤ Finally, any items which are missing or sent back must be acknowledged by both the receiver and the delivery person. In order to prove acknowledgement the delivery person should sign both the invoice and the 'Rec/Del by' column in the purchase and receiving report. The receiver should also sign the purchase and receiving report.

While checking the order for accuracy, the receiver should also check the quality of product received. If the quality of the product received is not consistent with that which the restaurant generally serves, customers may be lost as a result. All boxes of canned goods which are not sealed, or sealed boxes which are damaged on the exterior, should be opened and the cans checked to ensure that they are in good condition. A can that is bent may have a broken interior seal and, therefore, the product is unusable. All meats which arrive in vacuum packed/cryovaced bags should be examined to ensure that the seals have not been broken. If they have, the bag(s) should be sent back, as the product is likely contaminated and will not be safe to use.

Meats should be checked to ensure that they match the product specifications. If there is too much fat on the meat, the restaurant will be paying for fat which will be thrown out, rather than meat which can be sold.

Vegetables should be examined for freshness, size and quality. Old vegetables will have a shorter shelf life and may have to be thrown out before they can be used.

Additionally, there should be a scale by the back door. Every item which is purchased by weight should be weighed upon arrival. Even though some suppliers place a stamped weight on the box, the receiver should ensure that the weight is consistent with what was ordered and charged. In many cases suppliers pack ice or charge for the weight of the box in which the supplies are packed. Large boxes can weigh upwards of a pound and as a result may cost a significant amount of money on an annualized basis.

After the order is received, the receiver should store all the products. The first priority is to store the frozen items, then the items which need to be refrigerated and finally, the dry goods.

Storage

Inventory which is purchased by the restaurant should be stored in the correct environment in order to achieve maximum shelf life. All products should be rotated on a first-in, first-out basis in order to ensure the product's freshness. The Canadian Restaurant and Foodservices Association's National Food Safety Training Program and Food Safety Code of Practice , provide more detail on correct storage techniques.

Some of the more basic storage techniques are detailed below:

➤ All items whether they be frozen, refrigerated or dry stored should be placed on wire rack shelves and should never be stacked on top of one another. The reasons for utilizing wire rack shelves include: better air circulation, easier maintenance (spills fall directly to the floor) and better sanitation (moisture on a solid shelf will cause quick growth of bacteria and cause the contamination of food products). Additionally, there should always be at least one foot of space between the lowest shelf and the floor. This will allow for a more effective and faster cleanup.

➤ All freezers should be maintained at a temperature of 0 degrees centigrade or colder. Frozen food should be placed into the freezer before the food begins to defrost and should be kept where it is visible and accessible. The freezer coils should be checked weekly to ensure that they do not have a build up of ice as this inhibits effective freezing, increases the cost of energy and could cause serious and expensive damage to the compressor.

➤ While frozen food has a long shelf life it should be sealed properly to ensure that the product does not get freezer burn and becomes ruined. The risk of freezer burn can be reduced by double and triple wrapping all products.

➤ Never refreeze a thawed or partially thawed product without changing its state. If the product does not change state before refreezing, the product will be ruined and will not be fit for consumption. For example, raw chicken cannot be refrozen once it has been thawed, but previously frozen raw chicken can be cooked and then frozen.

➤ Refrigerators should also be carefully maintained. Items which need refrigeration are perishable and their shelf life is short. If storage procedures are carefully implemented and maintained the product will likely have a longer shelf life and there will be a reduction in waste as a result.

➤ In order to obtain the maximum shelf life, all products should be covered tightly with plastic wrap to eliminate air contact. To reduce cross contamination, never stack meat, fish, poultry or vegetables on the same shelf. Racks in the refrigerator should contain all of the same product vertically. Cooked product should be stored on the top racks and raw products of the same variety on the racks underneath. For example, cooked chicken should be stored above raw chicken. If the raw chicken were on top and juice from the product dripped onto the cooked product, bacteria would grow and food poisoning would be likely. This simple method of storage will assist in reducing cross contamination of food products.

Inventory controls

It is essential and cost effective for management to count the inventory on a weekly, monthly or four-week basis. Inventory counts allow the operator to:

➤ calculate the actual food costs for the period;

➤ determine the consistency of usage from period to period;

➤ compare actual and theoretical food costs in order to ensure that inventory is at proper levels;

➤ determine the accuracy of use;

➤ assess product turnover; and,

➤ compare food costs between periods in terms of dollars and percentages.

Unfortunately there is no simple way to count inventory. It is time consuming and labour intensive, but there are some methods which can be used to make it a little easier and less time consuming. Physical inventory can be calculated by using either the short form inventory report or the long form inventory report. The short form provides information as to the quantity and value of the physical inventory at a specific point in time. The long form provides this information as well as a record of the usage for each raw ingredient during a period of time.

When using the short form inventory report, management would calculate the inventory used during a reporting period by taking the value of the opening inventory, adding the purchases and subtracting the closing inventory.

opening inventory + purchases − closing inventory
= $ value of inventory used

The opening inventory is calculated by completing the short form inventory report at the beginning of the reporting period. The closing inventory is calculated in the same way. The value of purchases is calculated by totaling all the applicable invoices for the period.

Short form inventory report

The short form inventory report - closing count, illustrated in Exhibit 22, is completed as follows:

➤ List all items kept in inventory in the 'Ingredient' column. To facilitate the physical counting of the inventory, list the items in the same order as they are stored in the walk-in refrigerator, freezer and dry storage.

➤ Take the physical inventory of all the storage areas. It is best to begin taking the inventory in the large bulk storage space first, then the kitchen and finally the front-of-the-house. The quantity of product must be recorded in the 'Units on Hand' column using the same measure as used in the 'Unit Value' column.

➤ Calculate the value of the inventory. Take the latest invoice price for each item and multiply it by the amount of inventory on hand to calculate the extended value for each product. Add up the entire 'Total Value' results to determine the value of the inventory on hand at the end of the period.

When finished with the short form inventory report, a food cost percentage can be determined for the period by dividing the food cost by the gross food sales (net of taxes) for the period. Additionally, management can calculate an inventory turnover for the period by dividing the cost of food on hand by the cost of food used during the period. Food inventory in a restaurant should turn over approximately 36 - 42 times per year or a minimum of three times per month. A proper inventory turnover indicates that the restaurant is not carrying too much inventory in stock and therefore, does not have excess capital tied up. It also suggests that the stock is being used effectively.

Exhibit 22
Short Form Inventory Report

Closing Count			
Date _____		Counted by _____	
Period Ending _____		Extended by _____	

Ingredient	Units on Hand	Unit Value	Total Value

Long form inventory report

The long form inventory report, illustrated in Exhibit 23, is more time consuming to compile than the short form inventory report, but it provides valuable data which management can use to make more informed business decisions.

The long form inventory report documents each raw ingredient's opening inventory, purchases and closing inventory by units. This tracking provides a more accurate 'Inventory Used' figure and tracks usage of each item. The report will help management pinpoint problem areas and specific areas of food cost concern. Management efforts can then be directed toward the specific problem areas in order to reduce the restaurant's food costs.

Much of the long form inventory report is the same as the short form. The report is completed as follows:

➤ List all items down the 'Ingredient' column in the order they are found in bulk storage areas (e.g. walk-in refrigerator). Use the report to take the closing inventory in the same manner as the short form.

➤ Under the 'Open Inv' column enter the previous period's closing inventory. The closing inventory for one period becomes the opening inventory for the next period.

➤ Under the 'Purchased' column enter the purchases for each raw ingredient during the period. Transfer the 'Total Purchases' from the purchase log, described on the following pages.

➤ In the 'Close Inv' column enter the period's closing inventory.

In order to determine the figure for the 'Total Used' column use the following calculation:

opening inventory + purchases – closing inventory = 'Total Used'

➤ In 'Last Price' column write the last invoice cost for each item. The last product cost is used because restaurant inventory is turned over so quickly that the last price provides an accurate value for the goods actually on hand.

➤ To calculate the figure for the 'Closing Value' multiply the 'Close Inv' by the 'Last Price'. The result is the dollar value of each item on hand. Add up the entire 'Closing Value' column to determine the value of the inventory on hand at the end of the period.

➤ The 'Value Used' column is calculated by multiplying the 'Total Used' amount by the 'Last Price'. The total of this column is the actual food cost for the period.

Exhibit 23
Long Form Inventory Report

Date				Counted by			
Period Ending				Extended by			

Ingredient	Open Inv	Purchased	Close Inv	Total Used	Last Price	Closing Value	Value Used

➤ If management divides the sum of the 'Value Used' by the 'Closing Value', the result is the inventory turnover. Food inventory turnover in the restaurant business should be 36 to 42 times per year or three to four times monthly while beverage inventory should turn over 18 to 25 times per year. If a restaurant's results are lower than the three to four times turnover, then management is not using the inventory effectively, is tying up too much capital, and is not managing the food products effectively.

If management sets up the long form inventory report on a computer spreadsheet program, it will likely take only an hour or two longer to complete than the short form.

The value of the long form inventory report is that it allows an operator to track specific raw ingredients and create waste management reports on a per item basis. A waste management report will enable management to track waste down to the raw ingredient level and determine what action(s), if any, need to be taken.

Purchase log

As the long form inventory report relies on the tracking of raw ingredients, management must track purchases on a daily basis. This tracking is most effectively done through the use of a purchase log, illustrated in Exhibit 24. The purchase log is completed as follows:

➤ All the raw ingredients used by the restaurant should be listed in the 'Item' column. It may help to list the ingredients in the same order as on the long form inventory report (to make transferring the information easier at the end of the period).

➤ For each shipment received, the receiver should note the quantity received in the 'Quantity Purchased' column. The quantity received in the subsequent shipments can be recorded on the same row.

➤ At the end of the period, calculate the total received during the period and write this amount in the 'Total Purchase' column. This amount should be transferred to the long form inventory report in the 'Purchased' column.

Exhibit 24
Purchase Log

For Period _____	Compiled by _____	
Item	Quantity Purchased (By Unit)	Total Purchased

Sales mix analysis

The sales mix report, illustrated in Exhibit 25, is used to track the unit sales of each menu item on a daily and weekly basis.

The sales mix report details much of the information that is available from the cash register's preference report (which details sales by item). The advantage of the report is that it consolidates all the information for a period onto one sheet and allows management to analyze sales trends over an extended period. Based on this analysis, management will be able to:

- ➤ track trends;

- ➤ purchase more effectively;

- ➤ forecast sales and staff requirements;

- ➤ forecast daily prep based on anticipated volume;

- ➤ modify or design menus;

- ➤ assess and evaluate existing menu pricing policies;

- ➤ calculate theoretical food cost; and,

- ➤ match periodic usage in order to generate waste reports.

The sales mix report is designed so that the menu items are listed in the first column and the daily unit sales are recorded in the adjoining columns. The last column should be the 'Total' column where the total unit sales for the week are recorded. Menu items should be grouped by category (appetizers, main courses, desserts). A separate sales mix report should be kept for alcoholic beverages.

At the end of each week management should calculate the total sales for each product. It is likely that management will be surprised with the popularity, or poor sales performance, of certain products. Analyzing this report will provide management with insight as to the price points within which the restaurant's client base is comfortable. This information should provide management with guidance in pricing new items. Another important benefit of the report will be the ability to forecast and to determine theoretical food cost and product usages. These forecasts can be compared to the actual usage to determine the restaurant's effectiveness at controlling and managing inventory.

The sales mix report provides a sales history for the restaurant and should be the basis for projecting sales and demand.

Exhibit 25
Sales Mix Report

Week of Monday _____ to Sunday _____								
Menu Item	Mon	Tue	Wed	Thu	Fri	Sat	Sun	Total

Forecasting

Forecasting in the restaurant industry is the ability to project the product mix and/or item sales for specific days in the future. Forecasting provides management with the ability to reduce and control costs significantly through:

➤ more accurate purchasing;

➤ more accurate production of food by the kitchen; and,

➤ more effective and efficient use of staff.

In this section we discuss the process for accurate sales forecasting. In order to forecast the daily product sales mix for an upcoming week (e.g. the second week in July), management needs the following information:

➤ a daily unit sales breakdown for the past week (e.g. the first week in July);

➤ a daily unit sales breakdown for the corresponding week in the previous year (e.g. first week in July last year); and,

➤ a daily unit sales breakdown for the upcoming week in the previous year (e.g. second week in July last year).

The unit sales breakdown are detailed in the historical sales mix reports and the information is analyzed as follows:

- ➤ Compare the daily unit sales of the past week (e.g. the first week in July) with the unit sales of the corresponding week in the previous year and analyze the changes on both a percentage and number of units basis.

- ➤ Forecast the unit sales for the upcoming week by applying the percentage change (calculated above) to the daily unit sales for the upcoming week in the previous year.

- ➤ Modify this forecast to reflect new market factors. For example, a glowing restaurant review that is to be published this weekend will likely have a positive impact on the upcoming week's sales.

More detailed forecasting can be developed by comparing historical daily sales over the previous months (e.g. comparing the unit sales for the last 10 Mondays) and identifying trends. This is generally not necessary unless, for example, a new promotion has been introduced (e.g. Tuesday is wing night).

Sales mixes are remarkably constant from Monday to Monday, however, there may be bigger changes between days of the week and from season to season.

Forecasted sales will assist management in making better purchasing, production, and staffing decisions.

Theoretical food (beverage) cost

Theoretical food (beverage) cost is, as the name suggests, the theoretical cost of all food (beverage) items sold at the restaurant. The value of this report is that it allows management to assess how effectively the kitchen (bar) is controlling food (beverage) costs.

In order to determine the theoretical cost of sales, management must use two of the operational tools outlined earlier in this chapter. Standard recipes must be developed and costed, and an accurate sales mix report must be completed.

Once the sales mix report and standard recipes are fully operational, the theoretical food (beverage) cost report can be completed. Complete the report, illustrated in Exhibit 26, as follows:

> ➤ List all the items sold by the restaurant in the 'Menu Item' column.

> ➤ Detail the quantity sold for each menu item during the reporting period in the 'Units Sold' column.

> ➤ List the food (beverage) cost (from the standard recipes) for each menu item in the appropriate column.

> ➤ Calculate the total costs for each menu item by multiplying the number of units sold by the item's food (beverage) cost. Enter these amounts in the 'Total Costs' column.

> ➤ Calculate the sum of the 'Total Costs' column and write it in the designated area at the bottom of the report.

> ➤ Calculate the 'Theoretical Food (Beverage) Cost Percentage' by dividing the 'Total Theoretical Food (Beverage) Cost' by the period sales.

Once the report is completed, compare the theoretical food (beverage) cost, with the actual food (beverage) cost achieved, based on the physical inventory. If the theoretical and actual food (beverage) cost percentages are within 0.5 percent of each other, the kitchen (bar) has performed very effectively. While improvement may still be obtainable, management should be very happy with this result. If the food (beverage) cost differential is larger than 0.5 percent, it is essential that management concentrate on the kitchen (bar) operations in order to find out why the losses have occurred and to mitigate them as quickly as possible.

When discrepancies between actual and theoretical food cost occur, management should review many of the procedures outlined in this book.

> ➤ Over-portioning is a common reason for a large variance between actual and theoretical food cost. The simple over-portioning of a hamburger patty by just one ounce could result in huge losses over the period of four weeks.

> ➤ Free pouring at the bar usually results in excessive use of alcoholic beverages.

Exhibit 26
Exhibit 26
Theoretical Food (Beverage) Cost Report

Week of Monday _____ to Sunday _____			
Menu Item	Units Sold	Food Cost	Total Cost
Theoretical Food (Beverage) Cost			
Theoretical Food (Beverage) Cost %			

➤ Incorrect preparation of food (beverage) products can result in large wastage, which if not recorded on a kitchen waste report, will not be traceable.

➤ Staff meals which are not accounted for can result in large food cost variances.

➤ Theft of raw ingredients is common in the restaurant business and has a large cost factor associated with it.

When a large differential between the actual and theoretical food cost occurs, management should take notice and respond. Careful consideration and implementation of the controls outlined in this book will help alleviate many of these problems, while general awareness is of paramount importance.

Variance report

A variance report, illustrated in Exhibit 27, is used to check, on a daily basis, that the usage of certain key products is correct and that theft is not occurring. In order to use the report effectively, management must have in place standard recipes and a sales mix report.

The variance report itself is quite easy to implement and should only take the kitchen manager 20 minutes each day to complete. The report is used as follows:

➤ In the 'Item' column, list the products to be tracked. It is advisable to track the more expensive raw ingredients and to periodically change the products being monitored.

➤ The kitchen manager should complete the 'Opening Inventory', 'Purchases Received' and 'Closing Inventory' columns.

➤ The kitchen manager should then calculate and write the amount of product used (opening + purchases - closing) in the 'Actual Usage' column.

➤ The manager, or someone other than the kitchen manager, should complete the 'Theoretical Usage' column based on the sales mix report and standard recipes.

➤ Calculate the variance by subtracting the 'Theoretical Usage' from the 'Actual Usage'. The variance should be zero.

If there is a variance, these product variances should be recorded on the waste report (see next report). If this is not the case there is a theft, over portioning, short shipment, poor receiving, poor cooking or sloppiness in the kitchen. All of these problems are rectifiable and should be dealt with immediately upon discovery.

Exhibit 27
Variance Report

Date _____   Completed by _____

Day _____   Approved by _____

Item	Opening Inventory	Purchases received	Closing Inventory	Actual Usage	Theoretical Usage	Variance (in Units)

Kitchen waste report

A kitchen waste report should be maintained by the kitchen at all times. The report is important for tracking usage of the restaurant's food and it can also provide some very significant insight as to how the kitchen personnel are operating. One such report should be completed daily and be kept on file until the end of the period in order to track missing items.

The kitchen waste report, illustrated in Exhibit 28, is easy to use and is completed as follows:

- ➤ Enter the ingredient which was wasted under the 'Item' column.

- ➤ Enter the amount wasted under the 'Quantity' column.

- ➤ Provide a brief explanation of why the product was wasted in the 'Reason' column.

- ➤ The person who wasted the product or makes the entry should place their initials in the 'Initials' column. This allows management to follow up on the waste if necessary.

The report is used by kitchen staff to indicate what they have thrown out and why. Examples of the types of things which may appear on the report include:

- ➤ excessive fat on beef;

- ➤ products which have gone bad;

- ➤ outside leaves of lettuce;

- ➤ items returned by a customer (indicate why);

- ➤ product dropped on the floor; and,

- ➤ dishes that have been incorrectly prepared (wrong ingredients, over cooked).

Based on the information provided in the report, management can pinpoint areas of concern and take action to reduce the associated losses. Based on the examples given above, management may determine that there are problems with: purchasing, receiving, storage, description of dishes (either in the menu or provided by the server), training of kitchen staff, kitchen layout or kitchen equipment.

Exhibit 28
Kitchen Waste Report

Date _____

Approved By _____

Item	Quantity	Reason	Initials

Meal pick-up

One of the most important elements of cost control is ensuring that all food and beverage items which leave the kitchen (bar) are charged to customers. Unfortunately this is not always the case. Frequently the servers are so busy that they take a number of orders, bring the orders to the kitchen (bar), and serve the meals (drinks) all before entering the order into the cash register. When the customer asks for the check the server has to try and remember the entire order. In many cases the server forgets an item or two and customers will likely not complain if they are undercharged.

Accordingly, it is important that all food (drinks) be entered into a cash register before being picked up by a server. The kitchen (bar) staff should only make dishes (drinks) for which they have received a printed hard copy. This can be accomplished through either an automated or manual cost system.

The automated cost system uses a cash register or point of sales (POS) system with a remote printer feature. The remote printer is placed in the kitchen (bar) and the kitchen (bar) staff prepare only what is printed on the remote printer.

This methodology has several benefits, all of which have a positive effect on the restaurant's net income. First, it ensures that no one, including staff, gets a free meal (drink). Second, it ensures that all items are rung in, in advance of production, so there are no mistakes as to what was ordered. Third, it allows the service staff to spend more time on the floor. This will ensure better service and/or reduce staff requirements.

The manual cost control system is just as effective, but takes a little more effort on the part of the server and may not provide the benefit of reduced labour cost. This manual system uses a triplicate order system. When the food (drink) order is entered into the cash register, the order is imprinted on a triple hard copy guest check. One copy of the receipt is taken to the kitchen for the cooks, another copy goes to the bar for the drink orders, while the last copy is kept by the server for presentation to the customer. The three copies of the guest check are then matched at the end of the day in order to ensure that the information on each is the same.

Guest check control

Management should control and document the circulation of guest checks on the guest check control sheet, illustrated in Exhibit 29. Management should issue checks (pre-printed with control numbers) to staff on a daily basis and the staff should return all the used and unused checks at the end of their shift. The staff should be required to pay a high dollar penalty for any lost checks. If the restaurant has a sophisticated point of sales system, then guest check control will only be necessary during 'crash procedures'. The reason for controlling the circulation of the guest checks is to ensure that the staff do not bring in their own checks.

In order to fill in the guest check control sheet:

- ➤ Enter the server's name under the 'Issued To' column.

- ➤ Write the first and last numbers of the sequentially numbered guest checks in the column labeled 'Guest Check Numbers'.

- ➤ Enter the number of checks which have been issued in the 'Guest Check Numbers' column (it is helpful to issue guest checks in batches of ten).

- ➤ The servers should initial the 'Staff Initials' column to indicate receiving the guest checks.

- ➤ At the end of the shift the server should return all the checks that were issued. The returned amount is entered in the '# Returned' column and should be equal to the 'Number Out' column (this includes used and unused guest checks).

- ➤ Management should initial the 'Manager's Initials' column to indicate that all the checks have been returned.

- ➤ If there are any problems or outstanding guest checks, an explanation should be written in the 'Comments' section at the bottom of the guest check control.

Each day, the hard copy of the guest check should be matched with the kitchen and bar copies. This process should virtually eliminate any possibility of theft (free food being served to customers). However, in order to ensure that an item was not punched in on one copy of the check and not the other, the matching process should be completed. Matching is not necessary in an automated system, as only items which are entered into the POS are printed in the kitchen (bar).

Exhibit 29

121

Guest Check Control

Date _____

Issued To	Guest Check Numbers		# Out	# Returned	Initials	
	From	To			Manager	Staff

Comments _____

Beverage Cost Controls

The beverage area is one of the hardest to control within the foodservice industry. While many standard controls can be set up, managers are really at the mercy of their bar staff to ensure that all beverage sales are rung in correctly and that they receive all of the cash.

The major problem with beverage control is that, unlike food, one person in the restaurant has control over the entire preparation and service process. Bartenders, unlike the service staff, maintain inventory control, take the drink order, make the drink, ring in the sale and collect the cash. This creates a significant risk for theft, unless proper protocols are in place.

This section details several beverage cost control techniques including:

> ➤ purchasing, receiving and storage techniques;

> ➤ beverage ordering;

> ➤ beverage requisitioning;

> ➤ bin card system;

> ➤ bottle marking;

> ➤ inventory control;

> ➤ liquor control;

> ➤ standard drinks; and,

> ➤ beverage spill reports.

In addition, this section will introduce the reader to several new forms and reports. The following is a matrix of who is responsible for completing the various forms and reports, and how often each should be completed.

REPORT NAME	FILLED OUT BY	HOW OFTEN
Purchase order form	manager	2 times/week
Beverage requisition	bartender	daily
Bin card	manager	daily
Daily liquor count	bartender	2 times/day
Beverage spill report	bartender	daily

Computerized beverage control systems

In the beverage area, there are a variety of software control programs which can be used to monitor wine inventories and ensure liquor control. These systems range from the automation of perpetual inventories (i.e. bin card system) to liquor pouring and distribution systems which track ounce usage.

There are a variety of liquor systems which can control the amount of liquor poured through the use of electronic dispensing equipment. One such system has a ring which fits over a calibrated speed pourer. The ring will limit the volume of liquor that can be poured from the bottle each time. Therefore, when the bottle is tipped to pour the drink, only the amount coded on the pourer can come out. This system ensures an exact pour and, therefore, automatically reduces wastage and registers that one shot has been used from the bottle. At the end of a time period (e.g. shift, day) a usage report is produced which can be compared to the theoretical usage data generated by the POS.

There is another system which is used to monitor the weight of the bottles in order to identify over-pouring or theft situations. When using this type of system, management identifies the starting inventory and then inputs all purchases. At the end of the week (or shift if warranted) management spends a few minutes and weighs all the bottles. Each bottle's code is entered prior to being weighed and the actual usage is determined. The actual usage is then compared to the theoretical usage as detailed on the POS and detailed variance reports are printed. This computerization will save management a tremendous amount of time over the manual system described previously. However, the computerized system usually must be customized to reflect a restaurant's operation.

A more sophisticated and flexible dispensing system is called a 'bundled tower' unit. The system supports more than 100 beverage products and can dispense a variety of drinks. Orders are entered on an order entry terminal and the applicable beverage products flow from the storage areas (each liquor has its own line to the dispensing unit). The unit then simultaneously dispenses all the appropriate ingredients into the glass according to the restaurant's standard drink recipe. All the bartender needs to do is to garnish the drink. In many cases, especially a restaurant that only has a back-of-the-house bar where the servers pour their own drinks, this type of system should reduce both liquor costs (less over-pouring) and labour costs (less preparation time).

Purchasing, receiving and storage

The theories and controls for purchasing, receiving and storage of beverage products are fairly similar to those detailed for food products. One major difference, however, is that while a restaurant should purchase carefully and keep excessive inventory to a minimum, sealed beverages have a longer shelf life than food products. Therefore, if a restaurant has excess inventory, the product, while it may eat up interest dollars, will likely always be saleable. Another major difference is that in the beverage area, the forecasting techniques used for ordering are more basic and easier to implement.

Purchasing

Each restaurant should have two liquor areas. The main storage area, located in the back-of-the-house, is the stored liquor and can be accessed only by management. The second is the operating liquor and is used by either the bar and/or kitchen staff.

Beverage purchase order form

The beverage purchase order form, illustrated in Exhibit 30, is used to purchase stored liquor. The form is easy to complete and provides management with information for eight consecutive orders.

At the end of the reporting period, management will have a detailed record of what was ordered and what was used, all in a summary format which can be used for future forecasting. Separate purchase order forms should be set up for beer, wine and liquor.

Liquor should be ordered either once or twice a week. It is best to move alcoholic beverage products through the restaurant at least once per week. By maintaining a smaller inventory, management reduces the amount of capital tied up in stock and reduces the chance of undetected theft.

Exhibit 30
Beverage Purchase Order Form – Stored Liquor

INVENTORY																							
ORDERED																							
BRAND	I	O	T	I	O	T	I	O	T	I	O	T	I	O	T	I	O	T	I	O	T	I	O	T

The purchase order form for stored liquor is completed as follows:

➤ All the brands of liquor should be listed in the 'Brand' column. In order to facilitate the taking of inventory, the brands should be listed in the order they are stored. It may be helpful to also write down the container size (e.g. Absolut vodka 750 ml.)

➤ The manager conducts a full inventory count of the liquor in the stored liquor room and places the inventory numbers in the 'I' column.

➤ The order is calculated by subtracting the current week's inventory (I) from the previous total (T). The 'Total' is calculated by adding the 'Inventory on Hand' and the 'Ordered' columns.

➤ The order should then be placed in the 'O' column.

A restaurant can maintain this order system very easily and in essence it will allow for a floating PAR stock. A PAR stock is the inventory count of a product that should be on hand in order to ensure that there is sufficient product available between scheduled deliveries. A floating PAR stock implies that the PAR stock amount will be continuously adjusted to reflect changes in the demand for a product. For example, if there is a reduced demand for a product, the PAR stock is decreased, which reduces the quantity to be ordered.

An example of how a floating PAR stock works, follows:

➤ The first line is a restaurant's Absolut vodka. The opening inventory is zero and without historical information it is difficult to know how much to buy.

➤ Management indicates zero in the 'I' column and decides that 10 bottles should be sufficient and places that number in the 'O' column.

➤ The total 'Units on Hand' after the order is received is 10.

➤ The following week's inventory indicates that there is zero vodka on hand. This means that the restaurant has used all the vodka it purchased. As such, management can determine that the demand for vodka is greater than 10 bottles and purchases 12 bottles on the next order.

➤ In the third week, when inventory is taken, one bottle remains on hand. Management subtracts the one bottle on hand from the 12 ordered and orders 11 more bottles. The 11 are added to the one, providing a total of 12 bottles.

➤ 11 bottles are used again in the following week and management can replace them, keeping one on hand, or can reduce the order to 10 bottles, knowing that all 11 will be used without over stocking and without going short at the bar.

Conversely, if the second line is VSOP.

➤ Management has a zero opening inventory and orders 10 bottles for a total of 10 bottles.

➤ Prior to ordering the second time, management takes an inventory and sees that there are eight bottles of VSOP in stock. As management knows only two bottles have been used the previous week and there are eight bottles on hand, there is no reason to order additional stock for the coming week.

Management should reduce the VSOP stock until the inventory is reduced to a reasonable level and then reorder only to replace usage.

Beverage requisition form

Bartenders are responsible for ensuring that there is a sufficient supply of beer, wine and liquor in the operating liquor area. Near the end of each shift the bartenders restock the bar by completing a beverage requisition form, illustrated in Exhibit 31, requesting additional beer, liquor and wine from the stored liquor. The beverage requisition form (which should be a duplicate) is filled out in the following manner:

➤ The bartender dates the requisition and signs the 'Ordered by' line.

➤ The brand of liquor, beer and/or wine is entered under the 'Brand' column.

➤ The number of bottles requisitioned is placed under the 'Quantity Ordered' column and must match when the full bottles are brought to the bar and the bartender checks the 'Quantity Delivered' column.

➤ One empty bottle (for liquor and wine) must be returned for each bottle ordered and the quantity of the returns is written in the 'Bottles Exchanged' column.

➤ The manager takes the requisition to the stored liquor and checks off each item in the 'Quantity Ordered' column as it is taken out of storage and adjusts the bin cards accordingly (see Bin Card for more information).

➤ The bartender is responsible for checking that the liquor brought to the operating liquor area matches what was requisitioned. The bartender should then sign the 'Received by' line to indicate that the requisition has been completed.

➤ Management should break the returned bottles, or place them in a sealed recycling or storage bin, or sign the label with an indelible marker to cancel it, in order to ensure that they are not taken out of the garbage and resubmitted.

Exhibit 31
Beverage Requisition Report

Date _____

Ordered by _____

Received by _____

Brand	Quantity		Bottles Exchanged
	Ordered	Delivered	

Management should leave a copy of the requisition in the stored liquor room for future reference. The original copy is returned to the bartender and should remain at the bar until the end of the period when they are matched with the copies kept in the stored liquor room.

Receiving

The process for receiving liquor, beer and wine is quite simple. The receiver should ensure that the alcohol delivered is what was ordered and that the quantities and prices are correct. If an item is invoiced but not shipped, the item should be circled and marked as missing. The delivery person should initial the invoice agreeing with the short shipment. In addition, the receiver should advise the bookkeeper of the short shipment. In Canada, the majority of liquor, beer and wine prices are set by the provincial control boards.

Storage

All operating liquor areas should be locked when the restaurant is closed and the stored liquor room should always be locked. Keys to these areas should be assigned only to management personnel.

Similar types of liquor (e.g. vodka) should be stored together. The shelves should have labels indicating where each brand is stored. This will make it easier to find a specific brand and will facilitate the taking of inventory. Storing products in alphabetical order will facilitate finding a bottle and comparing bin cards to the stock on hand.

Wine should be carefully stored in a cool, dry and dark room in order to maintain the quality of the product. Wine which is subject to too much light or fluctuations in temperature can quickly go bad and become unsalable. Bottles should be laid flat to keep their cork moist. Once the cork shrinks due to dryness, air can enter the bottle and start an oxidization process that will quickly ruin the wine. In addition, if the cork becomes dry, it may break during opening at a table and the customer may ask for a new bottle. For proper storage of fine and vintage wines consult one of the many reference guides available.

Beer, especially draft beer, has a shelf life of two to four months if stored in a walk-in refrigerator with limited exposure to light. Beer made by some micro breweries is unpasteurized and has a shelf life of only two weeks, if stored correctly. The benefits of storing beer in a cold area are that the shelf life is extended and that the beer can be served immediately if required.

Liquor has a long shelf life, but this too can be extended through the use of proper storage techniques. Stored liquor should be kept in a cool, dark and dry area. In most restaurants the liquor turnover will approximate 25 times per year, so aging and long term storage concerns are generally not a major problem.

Bottle marking

Every bottle of liquor or wine which enters a restaurant's premises should be stamped. This stamp must be unique and difficult, if not impossible, to copy. Every time a new bottle of wine or liquor is requisitioned by the bar or kitchen it should be accompanied by the empty bottle it is replacing. Bottle replacing is a strong method of ensuring that every bottle sold is from the restaurant's inventory and bottle stamping allows for spot checks at the bar ensuring that only the restaurant's bottles are being used.

Inventory control

Beverage inventory control is different for the back-of-the-house (stored liquor) and the front-of-the-house (operating liquor) areas.

The stored liquor inventory is maintained through the use of a perpetual inventory system, called the bin card system. The system is very easy to use and allows for constant monitoring of all alcohol at a glance.

Bin cards

A bin card, illustrated in Exhibit 32, is set up for each item in the storage area. The bin card should specify the brand name, size (each size of a brand requires a separate bin card), and brand number generally assigned by the provincial liquor board. Every beverage product must be tracked on the bin card system, even if the item is to go straight to the bar. For each change in inventory the following information should be filled in on the bin card:

- ➤ the date;

- ➤ the quantity being added or removed should be written in the 'In', 'Out to Kitchen' or 'Out to Bar' column as appropriate;

- ➤ the balance should be calculated and written in the 'Balance' column;

- ➤ the manager should initial the bin card.

If a discrepancy exists between the balance indicated on the bin card and the physical inventory, it can be traced by matching the invoices and requisitions to the changes recorded on the bin card. If the discrepancy cannot be reconciled, the cross referencing will enable management to identify when the product went missing. As only a limited number of people will have keys to the stored liquor room it should be possible to assign responsibility for missing inventory.

Bin cards can be stored in one of two ways. It is easiest, space permitting, to place each item's bin card on the shelf next to the item. This allows for quick changes to the card. If space is at a premium it may be more convenient to store the bin cards in a three-ring binder.

A periodic check of the bin cards will allow for the constant monitoring of the stored liquor.

Exhibit 32
Bin Card

Brand				Size	
Brand #					

Date	In	Out to Kitchen	Out to Bar	Balance	Initials

Daily liquor count report

The control system for operating liquor is a little more time consuming, but is essential for maintaining control over the alcohol in the restaurant.

The daily liquor count report, illustrated in Exhibit 33, is completed as follows:

> ➤ The brands available at the bar are listed in the 'Brand' column.

> ➤ Each morning, the day bartender counts the full inventory at the bar and places the information in the 'Opening Inventory' column.

> ➤ Any alcohol which is ordered during the day should be transferred from the requisition form and entered in the 'Requisition' column.

> ➤ The night bartender enters the closing count and calculates the total usage for the day (opening + requisitions - closing = amount used) and enters it in the 'Amount Used' column.

> ➤ The daily liquor count report is then taken to the office for safe keeping and cross matching in the morning.

> ➤ Management takes the report in the morning and enters the theoretical usage (taken from the sales mix report) and enters it in the 'Sales Mix' column.

> ➤ Management then subtracts the 'Amount Used' by the 'Sales Mix' and notes any discrepancy in the 'Variance' column.

In addition, management should compare the 'Opening Inventory' with the previous day's 'Closing Inventory'. This will ensure that the bartenders are counting correctly and not adjusting for any improper actions which may have taken place during their shifts. Variances which are identified should be the bartenders' responsibility and they should be made financially responsible for all losses.

Exhibit 33
Daily Liquor Count Report

Date	_____	Morning Count by	_____
Closing Count by	_____	Extended by	_____
Variance by	_____	Approved by	_____

Brand	Opening Inventory	Requisition	Closing Inventory	Amount Used	Sales Mix	Variance

Standard drink recipes

Standard drink recipes are just as important as standard recipes are in the kitchen. Standard drink recipes should be developed and costed using exactly the same format as described in Food Cost Controls.

Standard recipes are important, as bartenders generally have their own way of making a mixed drink, especially exotic cocktails. In the final analysis however, each drink served at a particular restaurant should be the same from bartender to bartender. Additionally, in order to calculate the cost of drinks sold and to accurately match the sales mix report to the actual quantity of product used, drinks should be standardized in terms of portion, mix and garnish.

It is best to have all the restaurant's bartenders get together with management to review the beverage recipes and to agree on how the drinks will be made and garnished. Once the drinks are agreed to, they should be costed and placed on index cards. New bartenders, as they are hired, should be trained to make the drinks according to the restaurant's recipes.

The bar should be equipped with a second set of drink recipes (that don't show costs) on either a Rolodex or other indexed format. This format looks professional and allows for quick reference. Many point of sales units can modify recipes to print with and without costs.

Beverage spill report

The beverage spill report, illustrated in Exhibit 34, is essential for monitoring and controlling waste and spilled drinks at the bar. The report will help explain the variances identified on the daily liquor count report, as it accounts for each missing drink.

The beverage spill report will identify operational weaknesses and/or training needs. If a bartender is constantly spilling drinks, making the wrong cocktail or over pouring, then a training program may be necessary. In addition, the report will provide for a quick and constant monitoring of bartender weaknesses in the area of pouring.

A blank report is placed at the bar each day and an entry is made each time a bartender pours an incorrect drink or spills a beverage. This report should also show the overflow head at the draft dispensers. The bartender should write on the report the item spilled or ruined, the quantity spilled and the reason why.

The bartender should also be required to keep the spilled or ruined item at the bar for management to inspect. Once management receives a full explanation of why the incorrect drink was poured, they should initial the beverage spill report next to the item which was ruined.

In addition to approving the beverage spill report, management should physically pour the drink down the sink. This will preclude the bartender from selling or consuming the drink.

Exhibit 34
Beverage Spill Report

Date _____

Area _____

Item Spilled	Quantity	Reason	Staff	Mgr

Awareness

Awareness of what bartenders are doing is extremely important in maintaining and controlling a restaurant's beverage supplies. While most bartenders are honest, it is best to be aware of various 'tricks of the trade'.

Along with the paper trail controls outlined herein, management should have a general awareness as to what the bartenders are doing on each shift. While there are hundreds of 'bar scams' there are only limited sensible controls. Therefore, management awareness is one of the integral beverage controls. In addition, management should:

> - require all shots be poured with a shot glass which rests on the bar top;

> - not allow any bags, jackets or purses behind the bar;

> - insist that a sales chit accompanies every drink;

> - ensure that all beverage supplies are ordered with a requisition;

> - not allow staff members to buy or drink liquor on the premises;

> - only accept management voids which have a manager's signature;

> - display the U.S. exchange rate clearly at the bar;

> - ensure storeroom liquor is locked up at all times.

Unfortunately, there is not an answer to every bar scam, and as new controls are put into place, new scams will be developed. There are currently several methodologies to reduce the scam artist's ability to steal, and some of them are outlined herein. However, the most effective method is to be aware of the different scams that could be happening in the restaurant and be on the look-out. Inform the bar staff that controls are in place (even if they are not), as this deterrent alone may be one of the restaurant's best beverage controls.

Additionally, problems can be combated by making staff aware that management is monitoring staff performance and actions. Ask questions about what the bartenders are doing and be aware of any unusual behavior. If the bartender keeps moving swizzle sticks from one cup to another all night long, he could either be counting the drinks he is stealing or the revenue he is earning.

Labour Cost Controls

L abour costs are considered by many restaurateurs as the hardest of the three prime costs to control. The reason is that in making decisions regarding labour, management must also take into account the human element, labour regulations, and union agreements (if applicable). As a result, it is sometimes difficult to weigh an employee's needs against the expense incurred by the restaurant. In order to control labour costs, management should try to adhere to the following guidelines:

> ➤ minimize the amount of overtime paid;

> ➤ schedule sufficient staff to ensure that the restaurant operates in the manner that management wishes;

> ➤ maintain a fairly consistent labour cost percentage (labour cost ($) / total sales ($));

> ➤ create schedules which maximize staff productivity;

> ➤ ensure that the 'best' staff work the maximum 'non-overtime' hours and cover the busiest shifts.

These factors have to be balanced with the restaurant's staff requirements, the volume of business and the required skill level.

There should be at least some experienced staff scheduled for each shift. During slower shifts, experienced staff can be used to train new staff members and to supplement weaker staff. During the busier shifts, experienced staff will allow for a stronger operational presence.

Staffing in a restaurant is the science of hiring and assembling the correct complement of employees who are capable of functioning as a team.

This section will outline many of the components necessary for an operator to streamline staff requirements. As a rule of thumb, labour costs (salaries, wages, benefits) should not exceed 32 percent of the restaurant's total sales. This labour cost can be broken down to approximately: seven percent management salaries, 14 percent back-of-the-house salaries/wages and 11 percent front-of-the-house salaries/wages.

The labour cost controls covered in this section are:

➤ customer counts;

➤ hourly sales reports;

➤ scheduling;

➤ production standards; and,

➤ sign-in sign-out reports.

In addition, this section will introduce the reader to several new forms and reports. The following is a matrix of who is responsible for completing the various forms and reports, and how often each should be completed.

REPORT NAME	FILLED OUT BY	HOW OFTEN
Customer count	host(ess) or manager	daily
Hourly sales	manager	daily
Staff schedule	manager & kitchen manager	weekly
Sign-in sign-out	staff & manager	daily

Computerized labour control system

The most common labour control systems to be computerized are time clocks and payroll systems. There is a significant range in the sophistication of these systems, in terms of their capabilities and the extent to which they are interfaced with other systems.

Time clock systems are either 'stand alone' or interfaced with another system, generally the payroll system or an electronic cash register or point of sale system. In 'stand alone' time clock systems the accumulated labour data is manually transferred (through downloading or data inputting) to the payroll system. The time clock and payroll systems can be interfaced, allowing for the direct transfer of labour data to the payroll system. A time clock system can also be a part of the ECR or POS system. The capability of this type of system will be a function of the ECR/POS processing ability and memory capacity. The sophistication of time clock systems will vary in terms of the labour reports they can generate, their ability to compute net pay, and the amount of information they can store in the employee master files.

Sign-in sign-out programs have also been incorporated into several of the more sophisticated POS systems. As a result all staff (kitchen and service) can sign in and out directly on an input terminal. When connected to the central processing unit, the information can be used to automatically generate payroll information and cheques.

In selecting an automated payroll system it is important to ensure that the system can satisfy all the operation's requirements without requiring major programming changes. The system should have the capability of performing many of the payroll related functions described in this book, including: maintaining employee files; calculating gross wages/salaries, applicable deductions, and net pay; maintaining payroll registers (see Chapter Two); and, printing the pay cheques. In addition, the system should be able to produce all pertinent payroll reports.

In addition, labour and production schedules can also be generated by computer software programs. For example, one program currently available has multi-facility scheduling capabilities and can schedule labour, materials and equipment for the most efficient use of these resources. Scheduling can be done by department and work area within the operation while special options exist for scheduling specific tasks to be conducted by highly skilled staff. Scheduling can also accommodate last minute changes and flexible time increments. The program will print master schedules and provide 'red flag' warnings if overtime is about to be incurred by any staff members.

As with manual scheduling, the programs will take into account any of the variables which must be considered, for example: time off, vacations, sick days and so forth. The programs will sort these variables and generate a schedule that provides staffing levels that are commensurate with the service levels desired by management.

Customer counts

One of the most important factors in maintaining a reasonable labour cost is being able to schedule staff commensurate with the restaurant's volume of business. In order to do this, management should keep counts on customer traffic.

A customer count report, illustrated in Exhibit 35, should be filled out on an ongoing basis by the host(ess) or management. The report, which is broken into hour-long segments, provides a count of the number of customers entering the restaurant each hour. Management should also comment on any special events or situations which would impact these counts. The results provide management with valuable information with which to schedule staff and control sales.

By accumulating these reports, management can determine customer traffic counts at different periods of the day and identify different patterns in customer traffic between days of the week. For example, the period between 5:00 and 6:00 p.m. may be slow most days of the week except on Tuesdays when there is a special promotion. Based on this type of information, the manager will bring on more staff during the busy periods and have less staff on the floor during the slower periods.

Depending on the type of cash register or point of sale (POS) system the restaurant is using, the customer count report can be used to verify the number of customers that the staff indicated were at the restaurant. Sophisticated POS systems should track the number of customers that each server has. If the restaurant's system does not have this capacity, the servers should indicate how many people they served on each guest check. If the servers do not register the correct number of people, or neglect to register a whole table, they may be serving guests without accounting for the sale.

It is easy for management to calculate average checks for relevant times of the day. These relevant times will differ based on the type and style of restaurant, but the time frames may include breakfast, lunch, afternoon tea, dinner, and late night. The average check will assist management in analyzing server performance during different times of the day and will be useful in projecting volume. For example, if $500 of sales during a one-hour period is the result of five couples enjoying expensive meals, one staffing level is required. If the $500 is generated as a result of coffee and muffin sales, another staffing level may be required.

Exhibit 35
Customer Count Report

Date _____

Time Frame	Work Area	Total
8:00-9:00		
9:00-10:00		
10:00-11:00		
11:00-12:00		
12:00-1:00		
1:00-2:00		
2:00-3:00		
3:00-4:00		
4:00-5:00		
5:00-6:00		
6:00-7:00		
7:00-8:00		
8:00-9:00		
9:00-10:00		
10:00-11:00		
11:00-12:00		
12:00-1:00		
1:00-2:00		

Total for Day   _____

Total Sales   _____

Average Check   _____

Hourly sales reports

The hourly sales report, illustrated in Exhibit 36, is an hourly breakdown of dollar sales. This is different than the sales mix report which tracks unit sales for each period. Most cash registers and POS systems can generate a report which breaks down sales on a per hour or per period basis. The cash registers which only do a per period breakdown, break sales into, for example, eight periods which can be programmed specifically to match management's needs. If the register cannot compile hourly or period sales, management can determine hourly sales by taking an 'X' reading (total daily sales) every hour and subtracting the previous 'X' reading in order to determine the sales during the past hour.

Fill out the hourly sales report as follows:

➤ Fill in the 'Week Ending' line.

➤ Enter the sales for a given time period in the appropriate square.

➤ Total the sum of the dollars received during the various time periods in the 'Daily Total' column.

➤ Initial the end of the column to indicate who was responsible for the accumulation of information.

The hourly sales report combined with the customer count report will allow management to calculate the average check for a specific period. For example, at 10:30 in the morning a restaurant may get a large influx of people as a result of a coffee break in the adjacent office building. While the customer count may be high the sales may be low and the average check will also be low as people are simply buying a muffin and a cup of coffee. The hourly sales report will enable an operator to maintain a perspective on the customer count results.

Exhibit 36
Hourly Sales Report

Week Ending _____

Time Frame	Mon	Tue	Wed	Thur	Fri	Sat	Sun	Total	Percent
8:00-9:00									
9:00-10:00									
10:00-11:00									
11:00-12:00									
12:00-1:00									
1:00-2:00									
2:00-3:00									
3:00-4:00									
4:00-5:00									
5:00-6:00									
6:00-7:00									
7:00-7:00									
8:00-9:00									
9:00-10:00									
10:00-11:00									
11:00-12:00									
12:00-1:00									
1:00-2:00									
Daily Total									

Scheduling

Scheduling of staff is a very important aspect of the restaurant's operation and presentation. Through the use of a schedule, management must consider the level and quality of service they want to provide, while ensuring that excessive costs are not incurred. Scheduling is a delicate balance between service offered and the cost of that service.

When preparing a schedule the following guidelines should be followed:

➤ A schedule should be commensurate with the needs of the operation.

➤ A member of management should always be on duty.

➤ The most skilled staff should be scheduled for the busiest periods.

➤ Every effort should be made to avoid overtime pay.

Based on the information gathered in the customer count report and hourly sales report, some staff can be scheduled to work split shifts in order to maximize the coverage during peak periods. In many cases management may use two staff members when only one is needed due to an inability to manage the schedule accurately. For example, one staff member could be scheduled for a split shift covering lunch and dinner rushes rather than hiring two full-time people, one for lunch and one for dinner. This type of approach to scheduling may save an operator significant person-hours during the course of a year and, thus, will reduce labour costs and increase net income. Similarly, the use of part-time staff to cover peak demand periods can significantly improve labour cost. It is a waste of resources to have several staff, each only looking after a table or two, when half the staff could handle the remaining customers effectively.

Servers generally want a bigger section with more tables to maximize their income. This must be assessed very carefully during busy periods as it is counter productive to have the least expensive employees (the servers) be the bottleneck while the more expensive staff (hosts and cooks) are waiting for tables to be available or the orders to arrive. Similarly, a server with a big section has less time for service and suggestive selling, resulting in lower average checks, reduced guest satisfaction and lower labour productivity.

The staff schedule, illustrated in Exhibit 37, is used to coordinate the hours each employee will work and acts as a daily flash report of labour costs.

Exhibit 37

147

Staff schedule

Week of _____ to _____

Prepared by _____   Approved by _____

Day Staff	Mon	Tue	Wed	Thur	Fri	Sat	Sun	Total
Night Staff								
Scheduled								
Hours								
Average Wage								
Labour $								
Daily Sales								
Labour %								

It is easiest to have the management schedule posted in the office, and the kitchen and service schedules posted on the staff bulletin board.

➤ On the 'Week of' line enter the date of the first day of the week being scheduled.

➤ On the 'Prepared by' line enter the name of the person who developed the schedule. If the schedule is prepared by someone other than the management, then it should be approved by management.

➤ Enter the staff members' names in the 'Staff' column under the appropriate shift.

➤ In the subsequent columns enter the times during which each staff member is required to work.

➤ Under the 'Total' column enter the total hours scheduled for each staff member. This will ensure that no staff member is scheduled to work overtime and will provide management with a quick reference as to the maximum number of hours that each staff member should have worked.

At the end of the week:

➤ Enter the sum of all the hours scheduled on a particular day on the 'Scheduled Hrs' line. This should represent the number of hours worked in that particular area of the restaurant. The scheduled hours are considered the maximum hours worked as staff may be asked to leave early on a given day but rarely, if scheduled correctly, should staff be asked to stay longer.

➤ In the 'Avg. Wage' row enter the average hourly wage of the staff who are scheduled to work that day. While this amount may not be exact it should be a good approximation and will serve to calculate the day's payroll. Enter this amount in the 'labour $' row.

➤ Enter the total sales for each day on the 'Daily Sales' line.

➤ Calculate the 'Labour %' by dividing the day's payroll ('Labour $') by the day's sales ('Daily Sales').

If the lunch menu is different from the dinner menu, the above procedure should be completed for each meal period separately.

Production standards

Production standards take job descriptions one step further and are an effective way of reducing and controlling labour costs. Standards should be developed for all employee positions and should clearly identify the output levels expected from employees. These output levels should have two components:

- ➤ a detailed description of the employee's tasks and responsibilities (i.e. a job description); and,

- ➤ quantifiable levels of performance.

Examples of quantifiable levels of performance for the front-of-the-house staff include:

- ➤ number of customers served during a meal period;

- ➤ number of tables (and seats) that a server is responsible for;

- ➤ total sales per meal period;

- ➤ number of wine bottles/desserts/appetizers sold per meal period; and,

- ➤ number of turns per meal period.

Production standards can also be implemented in the kitchen as food is usually prepared in batches (e.g. stocks, soup, trimming or weighing portioned foods), therefore making it possible to quantify levels of performance. Examples include the following:

- ➤ the length of time to complete a specific task (40 minutes to prepare a batch of soup);

- ➤ a schedule that outlines when tasks need to be completed by (soup must be ready by 11:30 am); and,

- ➤ volume of production that should be achieved during a specific time period.

Sign-in sign-out report

It is imperative to monitor when an employee arrives and leaves work. If every employee charges just 15 extra minutes every day, a restaurant could end up paying thousands of dollars in additional wages annually.

There are several ways of tracking staff hours. The computerized time clocks offered by many POS systems through which an employee signs in and out are popular, but are not necessarily very effective. The biggest flaw with this system is that management is not necessarily there to verify the actual sign in/out. Accordingly, employees may sign in before reporting to the floor or sign out long after they have finished working. Also, there is the possibility that employees may sign in/out for one another. In addition, it is difficult for management, at the end of the pay period, to verify the accuracy of the time cards produced by the POS system.

Two alternatives to the POS system's time clock are a time card system and a manual system. Both these systems are simple and can save thousands of dollars. Such systems will provide management with an accurate account of when employees arrive and leave work. Management can make adjustments to, or write notes on, the time cards at the time a problem occurs. Additionally, management can maintain a daily record of hours worked which will facilitate compiling the payroll at the end of the pay period.

Under the time card system, an electronic time clock is used in which a card is inserted and the time is imprinted onto the card. When employees leave the restaurant they should take the card to management and have them initial and total the hours worked. By following this system, management knows who is working at the restaurant at all times, and knows when and for how long each employee has worked.

The manual system uses sign-in sign-out reports, illustrated in Exhibit 38, which should be stored in a three-ring binder in a locked office. The binder should be broken into key areas such as back-of-the-house, front-of-the-house, bar and management. The system works as follows:

- ➤ Each employee is assigned his/her own sign-in sign-out reports.

- ➤ Management controls access to the binder containing the sign-in sign-out reports.

- ➤ The employee reports to management to sign in and sign out.

- ➤ Management initials every entry and makes a note of any overtime.

- ➤ The employee also initials the entry as agreement to the hours worked and reported.

The manual system, while slightly more time consuming, is the best method to monitor actual labour hours and should alleviate the question of who worked when and for how long.

Exhibit 38

151

Sign-In Sign-Out Report

Employee _____

Week of _____   To _____

Day of Week	In	Out	Total Hours	Employee	Manager
Monday					
Tuesday					
Wednesday					
Thursday					
Friday					
Saturday					
Sunday					
Monday					
Tuesday					
Wednesday					
Thursday					
Friday					
Saturday					
Sunday					

Total Days Worked   _____

Total Hours Worked   _____

Gross Rate   _____

Total Gross Pay   _____

Cash Controls

While the preceding sections detail systems which enable management to monitor and control a restaurant's prime operating costs, consideration should also be given to the control of revenue and cash. Cash can easily be "misplaced", disappear, or be accounted for in different manners. Additionally, mistakes in handling cash occasionally occur and the results can be quite expensive. Accordingly, management should implement control systems to prevent both internal and external theft. This section concentrates on the controls related to:

- external cash security;
- bar floats;
- credit card sales;
- petty cash; and,
- bank deposits.

External cash security

External cash security relates to all the policies and procedures designed to protect the restaurant's cash assets from external theft and should include:

➤ Having insurance for the maximum amount of cash which is likely to be kept on premises (a basis for establishing this amount would be one day's total cash receipts).

➤ Controlling access to the safe by having only select people know the combination.

➤ Leaving the cash drawers open when the restaurant is closed.

➤ Bonding all staff who have access to the safe or keys to the restaurant. This protects the restaurant's assets from employee theft.

➤ Making frequent withdrawals from the cash registers in the front-of-the-house and depositing the cash in the safe. This is essential in restaurants that do a high volume of cash business.

➤ Making bank deposits during the daylight hours and always by a minimum of two people. This should reduce the chance of robbery while going to the bank to make a deposit.

Bar floats

In many instances bartenders are assigned cash floats for the bar. Each bar's cash register is assigned a float for which the bartender(s) using the register is responsible. The float should comprise bills in small denominations and coins. The amount of the float will be a function of the cash business handled by the restaurant and may vary between day and night shifts.

When a float is not being used, the monies should be sealed in an envelope and stored in the safe. In order to ensure that the float is being checked and counted every shift, and to identify the person responsible for the float, the bar float control report, illustrated in Exhibit 39, should be completed as follows:

➤ On the top section of the sheet, write the amount of the float and who/where the float is for.

➤ At the beginning of the shift, after counting the float, the employee should complete the 'Issued' section and sign his/her name in the 'Checked By' column. At this point the employee becomes responsible for keeping the float secure.

➤ At the end of the shift, management should count the float and then seal the monies in an envelope and store the envelope in the safe. Management should then complete the 'Returned' section of the sheet.

Exhibit 39
Bar Float Control Report

Amount _____ For Cash Register _____					
Bar Employee_____					
		Issued		Returned	
Date	Time	Checked by	Time	Checked by	

Credit card sales

In many restaurants, credit card transactions represent a large portion of total sales. In order to reduce the number of vouchers that are incorrectly filled out and thus not honoured by a financial institution, servers should be well trained in handling credit card transactions. In most cases, credit card charges are handled in a fairly seamless manner through the POS system. However, in some situations, manual transaction of credit cards are also used.

When using most automated systems, a server should process the payment as follows:

➤ Take guest credit card and go back to the POS system.

➤ Bring up the guest check and select credit card payment.

➤ Swipe the credit card in the 'reader' when prompted and print double copy (guest copy and one for guest to sign and leave behind). systems, usually for QSR concepts, no longer require a guest signature.

➤ Present the receipt to the guest for signature.

➤ Ensure that after the gratuity is added on, the server returns to the POS system and finalizes the transaction and closes the transaction.

In general, a server should process a manual payment by credit card (very important to follow this procedure in a POS crash situation) as follows:

➤ Swipe the credit card.

➤ Check the guest check against the bill to ensure that the amounts correspond, before presenting it to the customer.

➤ Authorize the amount being charged (either by telephone or by card swipe) and write on the credit card voucher the authorization number.

➤ Check and circle the expiry date, and if applicable, the card's validation date.

➤ Have the customer sign the receipt.

➤ Compare the signature with the signature on the back of the card.

➤ Initial the voucher and close the bill on the POS system indicating the method of payment.

While most credit card transactions are relatively seamless and automated, the latter procedures noted above are needed for those less sophisticated operations and in case of a POS system crash. In those cases where the restaurant is not automated then management should contact the restaurant's bank representative, who can provide more detailed procedures. In addition, each merchant bank will have specific procedures for depositing credit card receipts at their institution. Management should ask a representative from the bank to provide a training session to the employees and to provide a one page, easy-to-follow set of instructions for handling credit card payments and making deposits.

Management should also have a policy with regard to accepting personal cheques from customers. If the restaurant's policy is to accept cheques a series of controls and procedures will need to be developed.

They should include:

➤ Not accepting third party personal cheques;

➤ Not accepting counter cheques;

➤ Require picture identification;

➤ Record drivers licence number, name and address on back of cheque.

Petty cash

A petty cash fund should be used only for emergency quick cash situations and should not serve as a regular source of payment for supplies. Only management should have access to the petty cash fund which should be stored in the restaurant's safe.

The petty cash fund should be a set amount and should be sufficient to cover the restaurant's needs for a two-week period. The petty cash report, illustrated in Exhibit 40, is completed as follows:

Exhibit 40

159

Chapter Three

Petty Cash Report

From _____ To _____ Approved by _____

Food	Acc't#	($)
Total		

Beverage	Acc't#	($)
Total		

Labour	Acc't#	($)
Total		

Operating	Acc't#	($)
Total		

G&A	Acc't #	($)
Total		

Marketing	Acc't #	($)
Total		

Entertainment	Acc't #	($)
Total		

Occupancy	Acc't #	($)
Total		

Total Petty Cash Used _____

(Receipts stapled to back)

Each withdrawal should be detailed under the appropriate heading (e.g. Food, Beverage, Labour, Operating).

➤ The chart of accounts number and/or description of the expense (e.g. window cleaning), should be written in the 'Acct. #' column. This will ensure that the expense is charged to the correct account.

➤ The amount (including taxes) is written in the '$' column.

➤ A receipt for every disbursement should be attached to the back of the report. All the receipts should be dated and initialled by the person making the disbursement.

At the end of the two-week period, total each box and place the sum of all the boxes in the 'Total Petty Cash Used' line. The total of these purchases, plus the cash remaining in petty cash, should equal the original amount of the float.

Management should reconcile the petty cash to the receipts (stapled to the back of the form). Once reconciled, management should initial the 'Approved by' line and submit the receipts and the form to the bookkeeper for entry into the books of account. A cheque should be issued and cashed to replenish the fund.

Bank deposits

Each day management is responsible for balancing the daily reconciliation report with the bank deposit slips and entering this information on the cash receipt ledger. It is likely that the deposits will be made to different financial institutions (e.g. VISA and MasterCard may be deposited to different banks). Accordingly, good records should be maintained in order to allow the book-keeper to have an accurate and up-to-date cash balance position for the restaurant. The manager may wish to designate one bank account as being the main account for the restaurant and, therefore, transfer funds to that account on a weekly basis.

Management should update the bank deposit book (issued by the bank) according to the procedures outlined by the bank. The bank manager or representative will generally spend time with management detailing these procedures.

Chapter Four

Restaurant Valuation

Restaurateurs require valuations of their operations for numerous reasons, including refinancing, unit sales or purchase, or to assess personal net worth. While a professional independent valuation is usually necessary for refinancing, a restaurateur's valuation of his or her own business is usually sufficient for establishing a selling price and assessing his or her personal net worth.

It should be noted that there are many ways to value a restaurant and restaurant companies. The methodologies outlined here are the most basic and straightforward ways to determine a restaurant's value; however, there are many variables that have a direct impact on the ultimate value of any restaurant. The methodologies outlined herein can be used for single restaurant operations only and cannot to be used to value multi-unit, multi-national or public restaurant operations. In assessing a restaurants fair-market value, the one rule of thumb that must always be remembered is no matter the outcome, the value of a restaurant will never exceed one-third of the projected operating income for the balance of the remaining lease. So for example if you value a restaurant with six years remaining on the lease, the value will not exceed two times the adjusted operating income.

Fair-market value

The value of a restaurant should be based on its fair-market value. Fair-market value is defined as the highest price available in an open market between informed, prudent parties acting at arm's length and under no compulsion to act, and is expressed in monetary terms. This definition works best when the value is based on several restaurants being available for sale so that the buyer has several purchase options.

Additionally, it is assumed that the restaurant owner is not being forced to sell for any reason. Since the seller is neither being compelled to sell nor the buyer to buy, a transaction will take place only if both parties consider the value of the restaurant fair.

Financial evaluation

The valuation procedure outlined here is based on a restaurant's maintainable cash flow. In order to assign a value to this cash flow, the profit-and-loss statements should be formatted according to the *Canadian Restaurant Accounting* standards. Additionally, the cash flow should be adjusted to illustrate actual operating income and expenses only. For example, owner-operated restaurants occasionally pay management (i.e. the owner) a salary in excess of industry norms or fully cover the cost of an automobile that is not used exclusively for business. Such situations allow for greater operating expenses, reduce profit, and, subsequently, reduce tax liabilities. Therefore, each expense should be adjusted in order to reflect the actual operating costs only. As a rule of thumb, restaurants with less than nine years remaining on their leases cannot be valued at more than three times earnings under almost all circumstances. Restaurants with less than nine years remaining on their lease must be valued using a maximum multiplier of 1/3 of the remaining life of the lease.

In Exhibit 41, the apparent 20x1 cash flow (-0.3 percent) was adjusted to eliminate the inconsistencies that were created to reduce the associated tax implications. Additionally, costs that are blatantly out of control, like the actual food costs shown in Exhibit 41 (year 20x1) may be adjusted to reflect industry averages for a well-run operation. By incorporating such adjustments, achievable and maintainable earnings of $71,235, or 11.9 percent, can be projected for the hypothetical operation described in Exhibit 41.

The figure for projected maintainable earnings (i.e. $71,235) will be used in the valuation. Maintainable earnings are defined as the net income that a restaurant can be expected to earn on a long-term basis before depreciation, taxes, and debt service. The restaurateur should state all the assumptions used in arriving at the figure for maintainable earnings (i.e. indicate which items have been adjusted to illustrate the net difference between the actual and projected maintainable cash flows).

Exhibit 41

163

Chapter Four

Statement of Income and Expenses (hypothetical)

	Actual 20x0		Actual 20x1		Projected Maintainable	Earnings
Sales						
Food	$408,867	75.0%	$432,925	72.2%	$432,902	72.2%
Beverage	136,289	25.0%	166,662	27.8%	166,685	27.8%
Total Sales	$545,156	100.0%	$599,587	100.0%	$599,587	100.0%
Cost of Sales						
Food	$145,681	35.6%	$170,175	39.3%	$147,187	34.0%
Beverage	64,056	47.0%	112,261	67.4%	53,339	32.0%
Total Cost of Sales	$209,737	38.5%	$282,436	47.1%	$200,526	33.4%
Gross Profit	$335,419	61.5%	$317,151	52.9%	$399,061	66.6%
Controllable Expenses						
Payroll	$210,998	38.7%	$199,004	33.2%	$171,880	28.7%
Benefits	-	0.0%	$11,747	0.0%	$17,188	0.0%
Direct Operating	45,576	8.4%	10,896	1.8%	25,981	4.3%
Advertising	24,062	4.4%	16,699	2.8%	16,189	2.7%
Utilities	17,291	3.2%	5,712	1.0%	17,069	2.8%
Entertainment	12,503	2.3%	10,072	1.7%	6,000	1.0%
Administration, gen'l	32,438	6.0%	10,072	1.7%	17,069	2.8%
Business Tax	1,567	0.3%	1,645	0.3%	1,728	0.3%
Repairs, Maintenance	6,362	1.2%	6,222	1.0%	6,648	1.1%
Total Controllable Expenses	$350,797	64.3%	$272,069	64.3%	$280,671	64.3%
Occupation Costs						
Rent	$32,068	5.9%	$35,975	6.0%	$35,975	6.0%
Common-area Rent	11,180	2.1%	11,180	1.9%	11,180	1.9%
Total Occupation Costs	$43,248	7.9%	$47,155	7.9%	$47,155	7.9%
Net income before, taxes, depreciation, amortization & debt	($58,626)	-10.8%	($2,074)	-0.3%	$71,235	11.9%

Determining the capitalization rate

The capitalization rate can be determined in one of two ways. The first is to determine the equity capitalization rate based on the actual purchase price of similar-size operations. A restaurant would be deemed to be of similar size if the number of seats, target market, gross sales, and net operating profit all correlated with those of the restaurant for sale. The equity capitalization rate can then be determined based on the purchase prices of similar restaurants.

The second method is to determine the weighted average capitalization rate, which establishes a restaurant's value based on its financial position. This latter approach takes into consideration the debt-to-equity positions and principal paybacks associated with the purchase, and the maintainable net operating income of the restaurant.

These two methods are explained in detail below.

Equity capitalization rate

The equity capitalization rate is based on information related to the actual sales of similar restaurants. Therefore, the restaurateur is required to find similar-size restaurants with comparable gross sales and net operating income that have sold within the past six months in the same community as that of the restaurant being valued.

Once the similar restaurants have been identified, the restaurateur must determine the capitalization rate. First add together the purchase prices of each restaurant sold and divide that number by the number of restaurants used in the sample to obtain an average selling price. For example, if six restaurants were used in the calculation and the total of their purchase prices was $1,140,000, the average purchase price would be $190,000.

Next, perform the same analysis on the net operating income (i.e. the adjusted income before taxes, amortization, and debt service) of the same six restaurants. If the total operating income of the six restaurants totals $360,000, then the average net operating income is $60,000. The equity capitalization rate in this case would be 31.6 percent, as shown in Exhibit 42.

Exhibit 42
Equity Return

Average Selling Price	$	190,000
divided by Average Net Operating Income	$	60,000
equals Equity Capitalization Rate		.316

Weighted average capitalization rate

A more viable method of determining the capitalization rate is by calculating the debt and equity positions that a prudent buyer would take in a purchase situation. This debt-equity split is the "weighted average capitalization rate," and is determined by combining the weighted average of the return required to pay debt service (i.e. the mortgage) with the dividend, or return (i.e. maintainable net income) required by the equity component, which results in a capitalization rate that reflects the basic financial composition of the investment. To determine the debt and equity positions of the investment, the following factors should be considered:

1. It is common practice within the restaurant industry that the financing structure comprises 50 percent equity and 50 percent debt;

2. As a result of the high risk associated with the industry, restaurant investors require a high rate of return. They usually require a payback in approximately three to four years, which equates to a return on equity of 25 percent to 33 percent;

3. Term financing is generally available for restaurants at prime plus two or three points. Banks demand such a high rate of interest due to the risk factors they perceive as being associated with the investment; and,

4. A five-year payback of principal is generally required on a restaurant bank loan. Due to the short life of restaurant concepts in general and the fast amortization of furniture, fixtures, and equipment, the tangible components of a restaurant operation have little residual value after a period of five years.

Given these generally accepted principles, the restaurateur can determine the weighted average capitalization rate by using the following procedure (all figures are cross-referenced to exhibits).

Step 1. The projected maintainable net income is $71,235, as shown in Exhibit 41.

Step 2. The principal loan amount is calculated as follows:

➤ Estimate a selling price by multiplying the projected maintainable net income (cash flow) by three or four (e.g. $71,235 x 3 = $213,705).

➤ Assume that half of the $213,705 is debt. Therefore, the principal loan amount is $106,853. Round this number to the nearest $5,000 (i.e. $105,000).

Step 3. Develop a principal-and-interest schedule from a standard amortization table, as illustrated in Exhibit 43. Determine the annual principal and interest payments required for a five-year-term debt commitment.

Step 4. The total cost of debt is determined by dividing the combined total principal and interest payments ($142,254, as calculated in Exhibit 44) by the principal loan amount of $105,000. Therefore, the debt percentage return on costs is approximately 35.5 percent ($142,254 ÷ $105,000 = 1.355).

Step 5. As assumed above, that 50 percent of the purchase price would be financed. Therefore, the weighted cost of debt is calculated by multiplying 35.5 percent (Step 4) by the 50-per-cent debt position (35.5 percent x.5 = 17.75 percent).

Step 6. Also assumed that the other 50 percent of the restaurant's purchase price is composed of an equity investment with a three-year recapture period of 33 percent. Therefore, using the same logic as that in Step 5, the weighted equity return on costs is 16.5 percent (33 percent x .5 = 16.5 percent).

Step 7. Finally, the weighted average capitalization rate is the sum of the weighted cost of debt and the weighted equity return on cost, as illustrated in Exhibit 45.

Exhibit 43
Principal-and-Interest Schedule
(if annual interest rate is 12.75 percent)

Year	Principal	Interest
20x0	$16,068	$12,383
20x1	18,224	10,226
20x2	20,671	7,780
20x3	23,445	5,006
20x4	26,592	1,859
Total	$105,000	$37,254

Exhibit 44
Debt Return

Total of Interest Payments (5 year loan period)	$ 37,254
Total of Principal Repayment (same period)	$ 105,000
Sum of Principal and Interest Payments	$ 142,254

Exhibit 45
Determining Capitalization Rate Using Weighted-Average Concept

Weighted Average Capitalization Rate (17.75 % + 16.50 %)	34.25 %

Restaurant value

Once the maintainable cash flow and capitalization rate are established, simply divide the cash flow by the capitalization rate to calculate the fair-market value of the restaurant, as illustrated in Exhibit 46.

Exhibit 46
Fair-Market Value

Maintainable Cash Flow	$ 71,235
Capitalization Rate	34.25 %
Restaurant Value ($71,235 ÷ .3425)	$ 207,985

As a result of this valuation procedure, the fair-market value of our hypothetical restaurant is $207,985.

Using the weighted average capitalization rate together with the restaurant's maintainable cash flow is one method of establishing a restaurant's value. That value is based on the potential earnings of a properly managed business and allows for the required debt and equity returns. Although other methods of valuation exist, this procedure best combines the business and financial practicalities necessary to determine the actual fair-market value of a restaurant.

Appendix

Chart of Accounts

Account Name	Account Number

BALANCE SHEET

Assets (1000)

Cash	1000
Operating account	1001
Payroll account	1002
Sales taxes & GST/HST clearing	1003
Accounts receivable	1100
Trade receivables	1101
Employee receivables	1102
Allowance for doubtful accounts	1103
Credit card clearing - AMEX	1104
Credit card clearing - VISA	1105
Credit card clearing - MasterCard	1106
Credit card clearing - other	1107
Inventories - Food	1200
Inventory - produce	1201
Inventory - dairy	1202
Inventory - meats	1203
Inventory - poultry	1204
Inventory - seafood	1205
Inventory - bread	1206
Inventory - dried & canned	1207
Inventory - miscellaneous	1208
Inventories - Beverages	1225
Inventory - liquor	1226
Inventory - beer	1227
Inventory - wine	1228
Inventory – miscellaneous	1229

Inventory - Other	1250
Inventory - linen	1251
Inventory - china	1252
Inventory - cleaning supplies	1253
Inventory - paper products	1254
Inventory - glassware	1255
Inventory - flatware	1256

Prepaid expenses	1300

Deposits	1400

Property, plant and equipment	1500
Land	1501
Building	1502
Accumulated amortization	1522
Leasehold improvements	1503
Accumulated amortization	1533
Furniture, fixtures and equipment	1504
Accumulated amortization	1544
Automobiles	1505
Accumulated amortization	1555

Franchise Fee	1600
Franchise fee	1601
Accumulated amortization	1602

Notes receivable	1700

Notes receivable from shareholder	1701
Other notes receivable	1702

Liabilities and Shareholders' Equity (2000, 3000)

Accounts payable	2000

Deposits	2100

Sales taxes and GST/HST	2200
Provincial sales tax	2201
Provincial liquor sales tax	2202
GST/HST payable	2203
GST/HST paid	2204

Accrued expenses	2300

Bank loan & other short term indebtedness	2400
Notes payable	2401
Shareholder loan	2402
Bank loan	2403
Other	2404

Current portion of long-term debt	2500

Payroll liabilities	2600
Canada Pension Plan	2601
Employment Insurance	2602
Employer Health Tax	2603
Workers' Compensation	2604
Vacation pay	2605
Income taxes payable	2606

Long-term debt	2700
Bank loan	2701
Due to shareholders	2702

Shareholders' equity	3000
Common shares	3001
Preferred shares	3002
Retained earnings	3003

Owners' equity	3100
Proprietor's account	3101
Partner A	3102
Partner B	3103

INCOME STATEMENT

Revenues (4000)

Sales - Food	4000
Restaurant - food	4001
Bar - food	4002
Catering	4003
Takeout/delivery	4004
Retail food	4005

Sales - Beverage`	4050
Liquor	4051
Wine	4052
Beer	4053
Miscellaneous	4054
Sales - Sundry	4100
Sales discounts	4101
Merchandise	4102
Confectionery	4103
Miscellaneous	4104
Sales - Entertainment	4200
Cover charges	4201
Minimums	4202

Expenses   (5000)

Purchases - Food	5000
Purchases - produce	5001
Purchases - dairy	5002
Purchases - meats	5003
Purchases - poultry	5004
Purchases - seafood	5005
Purchases - bread	5006
Purchases - dried and canned	5007
Purchases - miscellaneous	5008
Purchases - Beverages	5100
Purchases - liquor	5101
Purchases - wine	5102
Purchases - beer	5103
Purchases - miscellaneous	5104
Purchases - Sundry	5150
Purchases - merchandise	5151
Purchases - confectionery	5152
Purchases - miscellaneous	5153
Salaries, wages & benefits	5200
Front-of-house salaries/wages	5201
Back-of-house salaries/wages	5202
Casual labour	5203
Management salaries	5204
Administrative salaries	5205
Bonuses	5206
Canada Pension Plan	5250

Employment Insurance	5251
Employer Health Tax	5252
Workers' Compensation	5253
Vacation pay	5254
Employee meals	5255
Employee social events	5256
Income sharing	5257
Other employee benefits	5258

Occupancy expenses	5300
Rent - fixed	5301
Rent - variable	5302
Property taxes	5303
Property insurance	5304
Business taxes	5305
Miscellaneous	5306

Operating expenses	5400
Utilities - gas	5401
Utilities - hydro	5402
Utilities - water and sewer	5403
Repairs and maintenance - building	5404
Repairs and maintenance - grounds	5405
Repairs and maintenance - equipment	5406
China and glassware	5407
Silverware	5408
Utensils	5409
Uniforms and linen	5410
Linen rentals and laundry	5411
Equipment rentals	5412
Contract cleaning	5413
Supplies	5414
Automobile expenses	5415
Decorating expenses	5416
Menus and wine lists	5417
Miscellaneous expenses	5418

General & administrative expenses	5500
Office supplies	5501
Data processing	5502
Travel and entertainment	5503
Cash over (short)	5504
Credit card commissions	5505
Dues, fees & licences	5506
Insurance	5507
Professional fees	5508
Security	5509

Telephone	5510
Capital taxes	5511
Bank charges	5512
Allowance for doubtful accounts	5513
Miscellaneous	5514

Marketing expenses	5600
Advertising	5601
Market research	5602
Promotions - external	5603
Promotions - internal - food	5604
Promotions - internal - liquor	5605
Promotions - internal - beer	5606
Promotions - internal - wine	5607
Public relations	5608
Miscellaneous	5609

Royalty Fees	5650

Entertainment	5700
Mechanical music	5701
Performers	5702
Booking agents' fees	5703
Piano rental, tuning	5704
Meals served to musicians	5705
Miscellaneous	5706

Interest	5800
Interest - notes payable	5801
Interest - shareholder loan	5802
Interest - bank loan	5803
Miscellaneous	5804

Depreciation and amortization	5850
Depreciation - building	5851
Depreciation - leasehold improvements	5852
Depreciation - furniture, fixtures & equipment	5853
Depreciation - automobiles	5854
Amortization - franchise fees	5855

Income taxes	5900
Current - federal	5901
Current - provincial	5902

INDEX

About the Author

Doug Fisher is president of FHG International Inc., one of North America's leading restaurant and franchise consulting firms with head offices in Toronto, Ontario, and affiliates in the US and Europe. With 25 years as an industry advisor and spokesperson, he is considered an international leader in the industry by his peers. This is highlighted by Doug becoming the only two-time recipient of the prestigious 'Award of Excellence in Management Advisory Services' presented by Foodservice Consultant Society International (FCSI), an organization representing over 1,500 consultants from 45 countries around the world.

His client base ranges from restaurant and franchise start-ups to some of the biggest names in the industry including, but not limited to: McDonald's, Quiznos, Tim Hortons, Dunkin' Donuts, Morton's of Chicago, Ruth Chris Steak House, Royal Bank of Canada, European Bank of Reconstruction & Development and VISA among others. His clients are based throughout Canada, USA, Europe, United Kingdom, Kuwait, CIS countries and the former Soviet Union.

Doug holds a Bachelor of Administrative Studies degree from York University, a Master of Science degree in Hotel and Foodservice Management from the School of Hospitality Management at Florida International University, and holds professional designations as a Certified Management Consultant (CMC) and Certified Foodservice Executive (CFE). He is a Fellow of the Canadian Association of Management Consultants and Fellow of the Hostelry Institute.

He has held, or holds, seats on the Advisory Board of Foodservice & Hospitality Magazine, George Brown College, Worldwide Board of Directors of Foodservice Consultants Society International, Canadian Association of Management Consultants, and Canadian Hospitality Foundation among others. Doug is the benefactor of the Fisher/Hollyer Graduate Scholarship for studies in foodservice management.

He is author of three other books, *A Guide to Restaurants and Bars, Successful Restaurant Strategies* and *Personally, I use my Spoon!*

Doug can be reached at doug@fhgi.com or www.fhgi.com or 416-489-6996.